This work was originally published under the title *Nuclear War in the 1980s?*

THE CHANGING FACE OF NUCLEAR WARFARE.
Copyright © 1983, 1987 by Ilex Publishers, Ltd.
All rights reserved. Printed in Italy.
No part of this book may be used or reproduced in any manner whatsoever
without written permission except in the case of brief quotations
embodied in critical articles and reviews. For information address
Harper & Row, Publishers, Inc., 10 East 53rd Street, New York, N.Y. 10022.

Created and Produced by Ilex Publishers Limited
29/31 George Street, Oxford OX1 2AJ

Research: John Pay of the Royal Naval College, Greenwich

Designed by Tony Gibbons

Illustrators: Tony Gibbons (Linden Artists) with
Peter Sarson & Tony Bryan,
Phil Jacobs, Mike Saunders and
Janos Marffy (Jillian Burgess Artists)

Cover artwork by Steve Weston

Color separations by Trilogy, Italy

Printed in Italy by Grafica Editoriale

Typeset by Optima Typographic, London

ISBN 0-06-055057-0
ISBN 0-06-096150-3 (pbk)

THE CHANGING FACE OF
NUCLEAR WARFARE

by Laurence Martin

1817

HARPER & ROW PUBLISHERS Inc., New York
Cambridge, Philadelphia, San Francisco, Washington
London, Mexico City, São Paulo, Singapore, Sydney

Contents

Introduction

Ever since the bombing of Hiroshima and Nagasaki the military scene
has been dominated by the shadow of nuclear weapons. Because those
two cities were effectively destroyed by what would now be regarded as
two very small atomic bombs and because even with "conventional"
weapons the Second World War implanted the notion that "strategic
bombing" means the wholesale destruction of cities, the image of
nuclear war is of a huge, death-dealing cataclysm, probably all
disastrously over in a few hours.

Mercifully this has never occurred and the actual global pattern of
warfare, of which there has been a great deal, has taken the forms
familiar earlier in the century, if embellished with many new technical
devices. Tanks, aircraft, machine guns and even poison gas have
produced latter-day versions of the two World Wars on a smaller scale.
Nuclear weapons have not, as some expected, "made war obsolete".

It may well be, however, that they have made it obsolete between
nuclear powers. We cannot know what the course of history would have
been without nuclear weapons but, prevalent though warfare has been
since 1945, there have been no wars directly between the possessors of
nuclear weapons and the two great nuclear Superpowers, the Soviet
Union and the United States, have managed to conduct a bitter political
rivalry of the kind that typically in history has occasioned great wars,
without opening actual hostilities.

This seems to confirm what those who did the early theorising about
the political consequences of nuclear weapons surmised: that the

The first atomic bombs were only with
difficulty made small enough to be carried by
the largest available bombers, and the fissile
material used could be spared only for the
most important strategic purposes. Today
material is relatively plentiful and nuclear
projectiles can be fired from ordinary
artillery pieces.

potential for catastrophe was so great and unmistakable that nuclear powers would establish a "Balance of Terror" between each other and then become very cautious indeed about starting a war. This balance would be very stable, because degrees of catastrophe are not significantly different. The only way nuclear war might begin would be by technical accident, mistaken and responded to as aggression, or by the appearance of a madman as leader of a nuclear nation. Both contingencies seem relatively easy to avert.

In immensely oversimplified form, those are the assumptions underlying the concept of deterrence that has been the accepted wisdom for most of the nuclear age. Now, in the 'eighties, this theory and these assumptions are being fundamentally questioned at all levels of debate. Quite suddenly, the confident theories and almost taken for granted assumptions are under scrutiny. The underlying technology is also rapidly evolving and what once seemed to be its unarguable consequences are now debatable. The idea that nuclear deterrence as we have been taught to know it is unsatisfactory, unreliable and psychologically intolerable is no longer confined to such groups as the British Campaign for Nuclear Disarmament; such disparate voices as those of President Reagan and Secretary Gorbachev are to be heard advocating the early abolition of nuclear weapons as a practical goal. If a careful hearing of such remarks reveals major differences in what future they prophesy or what means of achieving it, there can be no doubt we are in the middle of a fundamental revision of nuclear theory and a revolution in the possible forms of actual nuclear warfare.

The revolution in weapons that has characterised the latter half of the twentieth century goes well beyond the invention of nuclear weapons themselves and the remarkable changes that create the contemporary strategic scene owe as much to electronics as to nuclear fission and fusion. It is indeed the more recent advances in electronics that are doing most to alter the significance of the nuclear weapons themselves.

In its simplest form, the advent of nuclear weapons gives the possibility of wreaking destruction on an unprecedented scale. While there are practical limits to the size of fission weapons, the fusion thermonuclear or "H-(hydrogen) bomb" can be made virtually as large as one likes; the Russians tested a thermonuclear device yielding the equivalent of 58 megatons (MT) – that is, the equivalent of 58 million tons of TNT – roughly 4,000 times the force of the bomb that destroyed Hiroshima. Typical thermonuclear weapons yield one or two megatons and the destructive potential of blasts on such a scale are compounded

For decades the tank has been "queen of the battlefield", providing well-protected mobile fire power. Nuclear weapons present a new challenge to the tank, not merely because of the blasting power of the weapons but because armour provides little protection against radiation. Thus the most powerful family of weapons has become a potential factor even in hitherto "conventional" operations.

by effects extending even to genetic mutation. In very recent years a new fear has been the possibility of the smoke from the fires ignited by a large scale nuclear strike impeding the entry of sunshine, thereby creating a catastrophic "nuclear winter" in which crops would not grow for several seasons.

Nuclear weapons do more than create the crude means of destruction. By packaging the destructive power compactly – compare a single thermonuclear warhead with a hundred thousand of World War II's largest bombs – nuclear weapons, particularly the thermonuclear variety, make delivering the destruction infinitely easier. The H-bomb made the relative inaccuracy of early intercontinental missiles unimportant if all that was sought was the destruction of large urban areas. It is this combination of easy delivery with massive destructive power that has made defence against nuclear attack seem impossible and from that derived the basic strategic notion of the early nuclear age: that defence being impossible, the only security lay in threatening to retaliate in kind.

Such was the origin of the "Balance of Terror" and from that derive further ideas: that as all that was needed was the capacity to destroy an aggressor's cities, a limited number of nuclear weapons or a "minimum deterrent" would suffice; that there was, therefore, no need for an "arms race", and that nuclear weapons were in fact "militarily useless", because they were too dangerous to use.

Today all these supposed verities are questioned as the technological and political scene evolves. In practice, the war plans of the United States and almost certainly of the Soviet Union too, never envisaged the mere destruction of cities for its own deterrent sake. In addition to the so-called "Delta" or 'deterrent' targets, the Strategic Air Command contemplated "Romeo" or 'retardation' targets, calculated to slow a Soviet advance into Europe, and "Bravo" or 'blunting' targets, intended to reduce the Soviet Union's own capability to launch a nuclear attack. The last category in particular provided an increasing number of aiming points as Soviet forces grew and, contrary to the theory of minimum deterrence, revived the basis for an old-fashioned arms race, measuring force against force. At the same time, the increasing availability of fissile material permitted diversion to smaller nuclear weapons intended for use against tactical targets related to land and sea warfare instead of restriction only to strategic or homeland targets.

For a long time it was possible to argue that this continued "military" concept of targeting – the closely classified existence of which was for long in any case unknown to most of those who conducted public debate about nuclear weapons – did not make much difference to the idea of a "Balance of Terror", because the large numbers of big and relatively inaccurate nuclear weapons would devastate cities anyway, whatever their other purposes. But in more recent years, accuracy as precise as a few tens of metres over intercontinental ranges, has opened up the possibility of much more discriminatory attacks on precise targets, thereby greatly limiting "collateral" damage. In theory, this possibility undermines the accepted wisdom of nuclear deterrence. If the result of using some nuclear weapons need not be immediately catastrophic, then the motive for all-out nothing-to-lose retaliatory attacks is undermined, for such retaliation might provoke an "old-

The Soviet SS20 mobile ballistic missile, with a three warhead MIRV, represented technological upgrade of capability in the intermediate range so great as to open up wholly new, selective tactical options. This possibility of achieving clear dominance in controlling escalation up to this level of weapon, while avoiding such blanket devastation as would remove all NATO incentives for restraint, posed a fundamental strategic challenge leading to the much debated NATO INF response with GLCM and Pershing II.

Cruise missiles attracted most public attention, particularly in Europe, when US Ground Launched Cruise Missiles became the major part of NATO's response to the Soviet Union's SS20. They have been a technological reality, however, ever since the German V1 of World War II. Today, greatly improved motors, guidance and warheads have made them an accurate if slow delivery system for both nuclear and conventional munitions. Relatively cheap, they may be able to swamp air defences. Such tactics would, however, make careful "tailoring" of strikes more difficult than with ballistic missiles.

fashioned" devastating attack in return. Perhaps, then, nuclear weapons are not useless and unusable after all. Perhaps the great dilemma of NATO strategy is soluble. For ever since the Soviet Union acquired substantial nuclear forces, the American pledge to use nuclear weapons if a Soviet invasion of Western Europe could not be stopped by conventional means, has looked rather hollow, if the consequence would be an annihilating nuclear attack on the United States itself. But the threat of a limited nuclear attack might deter the Soviet Union without giving it the incentive to risk an all-out retaliation on the United States.

The possibility of accurate attacks with limited collateral damage also opens up the prospect of a duel between nuclear forces. Quite early in the nuclear age it became clear that merely acquiring nuclear weapons did not guarantee an effective deterrent; elaborate measures in the form of silos and submarines had to be taken to ensure the force was not destroyed before it could be used. A little later it was discovered that there might, indeed, be a defence against nuclear missiles; at least it proved technologically possible to intercept individual warheads. Thus it became necessary not only to be sure some deterrent forces could survive a "pre-emptive" attack but that they would be sufficient and able to penetrate any defences that might exist. Moreover, to do any of this put greater and greater demands on the systems both political and technological for controlling nuclear forces, a problem compounded by the fact that the electromagnetic pulses from nuclear explosions can severely disrupt electronic processes. As a consequence one of the most intense areas of military investment today is in "C^3I", command, communication, control and intelligence.

By the late 'eighties, the outlines of the nuclear strategic scene, until recently commonly believed to be fixed and simple if terrifying, are shifting and blurred. The consequences are ambiguous; on the one hand nuclear weapons seem to be becoming at least theoretically more usable and more "useful" for strategic purposes. On the other hand, this very prospect breeds a hankering after the old stability and the hope that if that is not emerging from the spontaneous evolution of technology it must be imposed by sweeping arms control. One particular area of swiftly advancing technology, that concerned with strategic defences or "Starwars", exemplifies this ambiguity, for defences might make it possible to live with inevitably less than perfect measures to limit offensive weapons but could also be used as part of a sophisticated apparatus for fighting "limited" nuclear wars.

So complex is the politico-strategic system that it is not even clear which of these alternative strategic worlds would be the safer. What does seem certain is that the next few years will see dramatic developments in the technology, strategy and politics of the nuclear balance. The components of that balance are the subject of the following pages.

The picture gives an artist's impression of some modern delivery systems for conventional weapons. Cluster weapons, some of which contain individually guided sub-munitions, others depending on a "statistical" pattern, are launched by aircraft in a hotly contested airspace. Minelets are scattered to impede and destroy both troops and vehicles. Similar techniques can be employed by other delivery systems, such as Multiple Launch Rocket Systems (MLRS) and novel munitions such as fuel-air explosives could be employed as well as chemical weapons. Such developments give "conventional" weapons new competitiveness with nuclear weapons in tactical uses; but this is only achieved at considerable cost.

The Evolving Nuclear Scene

Technology and Doctrine

The central source of the nuclear revolutionising of the strategic scene is the ability to create immensely damaging explosions which add to the conventional explosive effects of blast and heat the new phenomena associated with radiation. A military nuclear force is, however, much more than simply nuclear explosives; though necessary, these are far from sufficient and in terms of cost and technological complexity the actual nuclear warheads are a minor part of the whole.

Effective nuclear forces must have the means to identify their targets and deliver weapons accurately to them. This entails the ready availability of the force to act; consequently it must be reasonably proof against attack. From this arises a need for warning systems and methods of self-protection: the latter may range from "launch-on-warning" — irreversible for ballistic missiles — to hardening, hiding or mobility. When the only long-range means of delivery was aircraft, the ability entailed the need to penetrate air defences. At first ballistic missiles enjoyed a "free ride" once launched, but now there are several theoretical and a few already realised means of interception; hence the increasing need for "penetration aids" (PENAIDS) including decoy re-entry vehicles (RV), electronic countermeasures (ECM), hardening of RVs, and renewed interest in the air breathing alternatives to ballistic missiles.

In the early days of the nuclear age, making a nuclear force more powerful was likely to be thought of in terms of more and more powerful warheads. Today the accuracy of delivery makes those variables less interesting than the overall reliability and flexibility of the force, qualities arising from the careful combination of all the elements of a weapon system and its integration into a strategic concept. One reason why the process of proliferation of weapons to new nuclear powers has been much slower than once feared is undoubtedly the rising cost of keeping up with the pace of technology. On the other hand, in simple cost of destructive power, nuclear weapons can be much cheaper than the immensely expensive sophisticated conventional forces of today. In a very real sense the notorious idea of "more bang for a buck" is true.

In practice, nuclear weapons have to be considered in combination with conventional forces to arrive at a coherent strategy. The task of harnessing nuclear power to useful strategies and hence to the service of national security policy is a difficult one. Such a powerful instrument is not easy to control. Perceptions of this and of the dangers of failure have given unprecedented dominance to arms control issues on the diplomatic scene.

Compared with pre-war years, the achievements of arms control negotiations in recent years have been remarkable and this is now an ever-present element in the practice and politics of nuclear strategy. Measured by the scale of the problem, however, arms control has made only hesitant and not always positive steps. At the end of the 1980s it is difficult to decide whether we are on the eve of a golden age of arms control or of an arms race reaching from underseas to outer space.

An impression of the coverage provided by American early warning radars. The ABM Treaty requires this coverage to be provided facing outwards from national peripheries so as not to provide battle management capability for ABM defence. Three Ballistic Missile Early Warning Systems (BMEWS) in Alaska, Greenland and the UK are left over from an earlier period, but a controversial modernisation programme to phased array is now in contemplation.

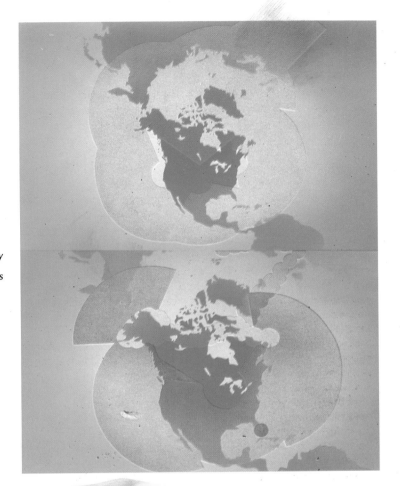

US radar coverage against air attack, a facility somewhat neglected while Soviet bomber forces were weak, but now more essential as the Soviet Union acquires new aircraft and cruise missiles. New Over the Horizon (OTH) radars provide cover out to 1800 miles.

A modern US radar station in the north with phased arrays replacing the more familiar mechanically rotated antennae. Warning is one of the most vital elements in determining the effectiveness of a defence as time eases the demands on the interceptor system.

1 Early warning system detects nuclear attack.

2 NORAD confirms nuclear attack alert. Chiefs of staff and President informed.

3 Strategic air command bomber crews, ICBM's and SLBM's on full alert.

4 President consults with chiefs of staff. Final confirmation of nuclear attack.

5 Nuclear-armed strategic air command bombers take off.

6 SLBM's are launched from submarines.

Surprise Attack

Surprise is always a valuable advantage in war. Where strategic nuclear weapons are involved, this advantage could be essential, for in the absence of any really adequate active defences as shelter against nuclear weapons, the only way to reduce the enemy's capacity to do devastating damage is to catch his offensive forces before they are used. Such an attack could be launched "out of the blue" in a "preventive" war but it is generally assumed that commanders would only take such a drastic and risky step if they believed they were actually about to be attacked themselves; in such a case they might indeed mount what is termed a "pre-emptive" attack.

In aerial warfare surprise has a long history of at least partial success: Germany in 1939 and 1940 against Poland and France, Japan in the classic Pearl Harbor attack of 1941, and the decisive Israeli elimination of the Arab forces in 1967.

A would-be deterrent retaliatory nuclear force must, therefore, make every effort possible to be "survivable" and to preserve a "secure second strike". There are numerous approaches to this problem: hardening weapons and bases, concealing them, making them mobile,

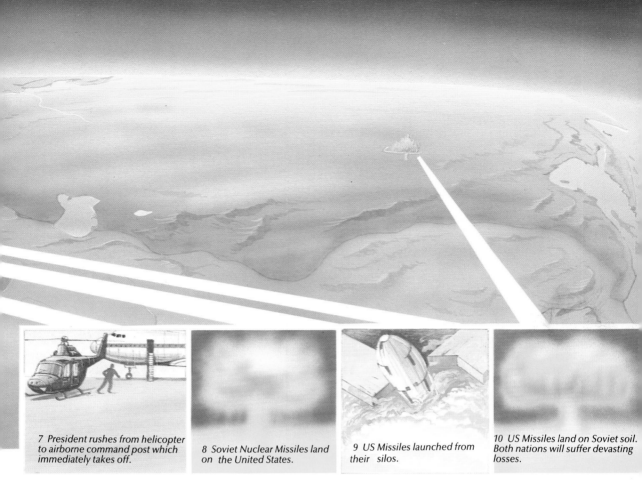

7 President rushes from helicopter to airborne command post which immediately takes off.

8 Soviet Nuclear Missiles land on the United States.

9 US Missiles launched from their silos.

10 US Missiles land on Soviet soil. Both nations will suffer devasting losses.

perhaps as in the case of aircraft by airborne alert at times of crisis. It is, of course, not enough to preserve just the weapons; the apparatus of command and control must also be safeguarded from the political leadership down to the firing command posts and the weapons themselves. Given an attack by ballistic missiles, there may be at most 30 minutes to achieve all this; ballistic missiles fired on depressed trajectory at short-range may reduce this to little more than 10 minutes.

Fixed land based missiles have the disadvantage of being almost certainly vulnerable if retained on base, but the policy of "launch on warning" is obviously a dangerous one, putting a special premium on the accuracy of warning. A nuclear balance may be much more stable, consequently, if the retaliatory force can ride out an attack.

The capacity of many weapons to do this — submarine launched weapons for instance — has led some to suggest a surprise attack could never be sensible. But much depends on circumstances. A nuclear power that had lost many of its weapons, particularly the more accurate land based ones, yet had its cities spared, might be no longer able to launch an effective "counter-force" attack in kind, and be very unwise to attack enemy cities and thereby provoke the loss of its own. Retaining as flexible a force as possible after a surprise attack remains an important strategic goal.

Triad

Although various nuclear weapons systems have special advantages for attacking different types of target — ballistic missiles can penetrate active defences, aircraft crews can seek out imprecisely located targets — it is the need for "survivability" that has most impelled nuclear powers to maintain a mix of delivery vehicles. Roughly speaking these form a "triad" of aircraft and cruise missiles (CM), land based intercontinental ballistic missiles (ICBM), and sea based, usually submarine launched missiles (SLBM).

Each of these systems has its own advantages and disadvantages but the principle of variety has intrinsic merits of its own. In the first place, diversity in ways of basing weapons complicates an attacker's problem; he too needs a variety of offensive methods — anti-submarine techniques, for instance, as well as offensive warheads — and faces compounded problems in timing his attack; using aircraft to locate mobile missiles, for example, would greatly extend warning time for command systems to gear up and dispersible weapons to do so. Less obviously, a variety of retaliatory vehicles minimises the consequences if one type proves unexpectedly vulnerable or inefficient.

Manned Bombers The "original" vehicle for strategic attack, predating the nuclear age, bombers have high payload, potentially high accuracy, good reconnaissance and attack reporting capability, and the invaluable quality of "recallability". They are, however, vulnerable to active defences and to pre-emptive attack on the ground. To deal partially with the latter they can be placed in hardened hangarettes or put on (expensive) airborne alert. Like cruise missiles, with which they share many characteristics, they have a long flight time and therefore give prolonged warning. Stealth technology (see pages 40-41) may remedy this.

ICBMs Fastest reacting weapons, most easily controlled and accurate of the ballistic systems, ICBMs are vulnerable in fixed bases; even hardening in silos is difficult against the latest achievable accuracy of offensive missiles, though the task of completely eliminating a large ICBM force is no easy one. ICBMs can be made mobile on trucks or trains; this raises political problems at least in the democracies but current American plans call for dispersal on large military bases.

SLBMs Putting missiles to sea on submarines is so far regarded as virtually solving the problem of pre-launch vulnerability. Hitherto SLBMs have had reduced accuracy (because of imprecise location of the submarine) and have been difficult to communicate with while maintaining deeply submerged security; impending technological advances will greatly improve accuracy (Trident II) and do something to improve C^3.

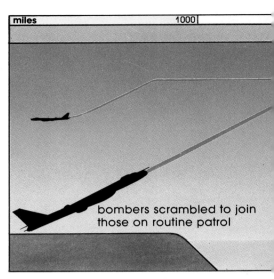

bombers scrambled to join those on routine patrol

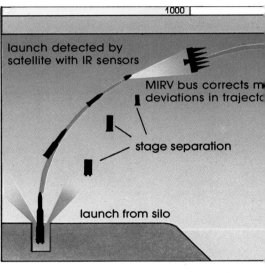

launch detected by satellite with IR sensors

MIRV bus corrects m deviations in trajecto

stage separation

launch from silo

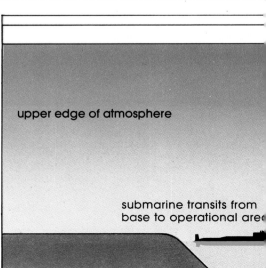

upper edge of atmosphere

submarine transits from base to operational are

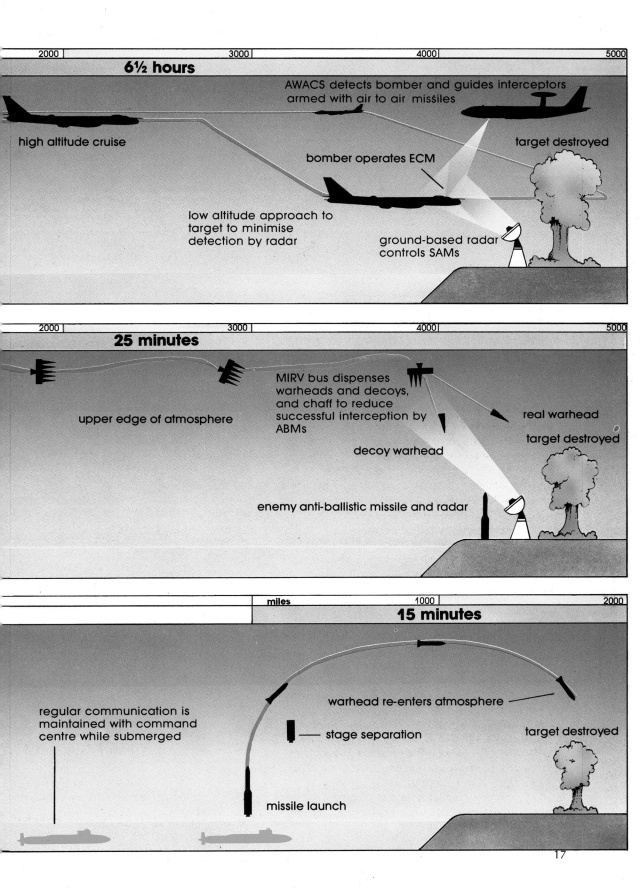

6½ hours

2000 · 3000 · 4000 · 5000

high altitude cruise

AWACS detects bomber and guides interceptors
armed with air to air missiles

target destroyed

bomber operates ECM

low altitude approach to
target to minimise
detection by radar

ground-based radar
controls SAMs

25 minutes

2000 · 3000 · 4000 · 5000

upper edge of atmosphere

MIRV bus dispenses
warheads and decoys,
and chaff to reduce
successful interception by
ABMs

real warhead

target destroyed

decoy warhead

enemy anti-ballistic missile and radar

15 minutes

miles · 1000 · 2000

regular communication is
maintained with command
centre while submerged

warhead re-enters atmosphere

stage separation

target destroyed

missile launch

17

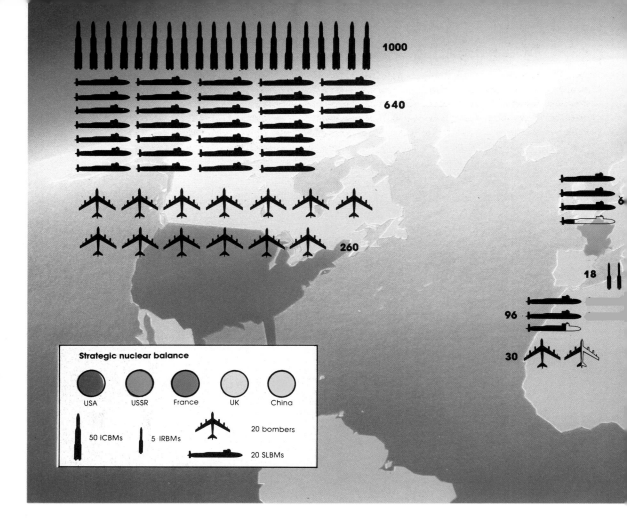

Strategic nuclear balance

USA USSR France UK China

50 ICBMs   5 IRBMs   20 bombers   20 SLBMs

Nuclear Arsenals

The world contains five declared nuclear powers: the Soviet Union, the United States, China, France and the United Kingdom. Of the five, the two Superpowers maintain forces on a vastly greater scale than the other three.

Each of the Superpowers deploys a triad of strategic weapons (many more weapons not counted here are dedicated to tactical or theatre use in regional military balances — some of these could be applied to "strategic" uses and vice versa). China and France maintain at least the semblance of a triad, though the Chinese force is still technologically backward. British strategic power depends entirely on SLBMs, currently Polaris with a British re-entry vehicle, Chevaline, and prospectively Trident II acquired, like Polaris, from the United States.

While both Superpowers maintain the triad of land, sea and air-launched weapons, the mix is different, reflecting different geopolitical circumstances and strategic philosophy. Originally, the American force was dominated by the air force and bombers still have a major role; Soviet aircraft have been less significant, though the gross numbers are significant, and the strategic forces have been characterised by an

While delivery vehicles are only one measure of nuclear power, they are not merely important in themselves, but one of the prime categories seized upon by designers of arms control agreements because of their relative visibility and hence amenability to verification. The map dramatises the immense disparity between the forces of the Superpowers and the other nuclear states.

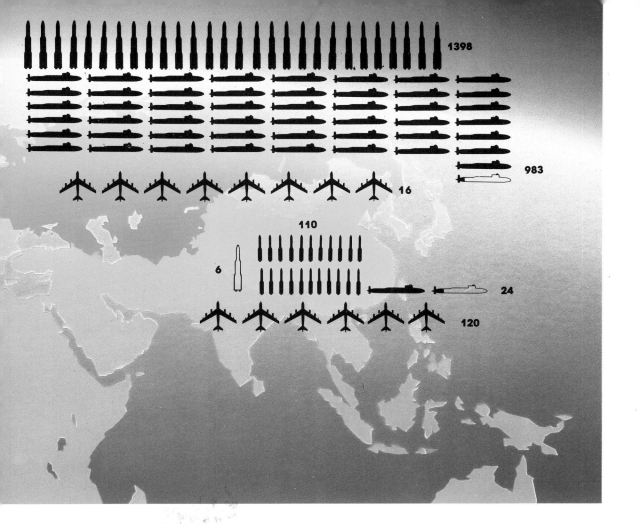

1398

983

16

110

6

24

120

"artillery" approach, emphasising ICBMs for which the vast, secretive Soviet land mass is highly suitable. In keeping with this approach, the Soviet Union has moved most actively toward mobile land based missiles as a solution to increasing fixed ICBM vulnerability.

Growth in the number of nuclear weapons has been primarily driven by the desire to have a "counterforce" capability against the enemy, so as to achieve "damage limitation" for oneself; adequate capability to destroy cities was achieved long ago, so long as the retaliatory force was thought survivable. Even when the goal of disarming the enemy by pre-emption has been thought probably unattainable, multiplication of weapons has proceeded in order to multiply "aimpoints" and thereby reduce the enemy's chance of successful counterforce. In recent years, American strategists have become more interested in the capacity to destroy key elements in the Soviet war and recovery potential rather than the crude destruction of cities. This doctrine, which may always have been important in Soviet theory, tends to increase the need for numerous warheads but to reduce the size required. The lesser nuclear powers have not been able to afford such refinements and have concentrated on maintaining a reliable "city busting" capability.

19

Superpower Arsenals

Estimated Strategic Nuclear Warheads USA

System	Number deployed	Total warheads
Minuteman II		
Minuteman III		
MX		
SLBM Poseidon C-3		
Trident C-4		
Sub-total	1,640	7,802
Aircraft B-52G		
B-52H		
FB-111A		
TOTAL:	1,937	11,466

Accepting that the rational political purpose of a nuclear force must be to deter war and preserve national security, its fundamental military role is to explode warheads on targets. The gross number and power of warheads is thus an important measure of a nuclear force and one of which a rough estimate can be made.

This is, however, only a crude measure. Only warheads that arrive on target are effective. Moreover, that effectiveness must be measured not in gross explosive power but in terms of adequacy to do the required degree of damage. Furthermore the value of such damage to the force inflicting it depends on the importance of the target, its place in the strategy of the attacker, and ultimately on the efficacy of the strategy. Recent refinement of American strategy has led to force modernisation being accompanied by a fall in both the number and the power of warheads; the yield of the total stockpile has fallen by a factor of four and the number of weapons by a third. The resulting force is, however, believed to be more and not less effective.

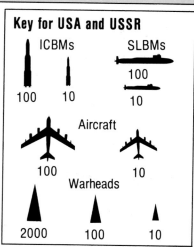

Key for USA and USSR

ICBMs — 100, 10

SLBMs — 100, 10

Aircraft — 100, 10

Warheads — 2000, 100, 10

Estimated Strategic Nuclear Warheads USSR

System	Number deployed	Total warheads
ICBM SS-11		
SS-13		
SS-17		
SS-18		
SS-19		
SS-25		
SLBM SS-N-5		
SS-N-6		
SS-N-8		
SS-NX-17		
SS-N-18		
SS-N-20		
SS-N-23		
Sub-total	2,381	10,201
Aircraft Tu-95		
Mya-4		
Tu-22M		
TOTAL:	2,801	11,241

Reliability

Reliability is a highly desirable characteristic of any technological device and particularly of weapons upon which issues of life and death depend. In the case of nuclear weapons, reliability is peculiarly essential because of the magnitude of the consequences of use or malfunction. Moreover, where nuclear weapons are used in a policy of deterrence, a high degree of assurance that the weapons would have their intended effect is an intrinsic part of the strategic concept. This is true, even though the person deterred may be particularly reluctant to test any suspicion he may have that the deterrent system will not work well, for while this caution may be a salutary feature of nuclear balances, there can be no value in deliberately eroding the caution by depending upon unreliable weapons. Of course there remains the separate question of how much is known about reliability; once again, however, it would be unwise to let the possibility of an enemy having exaggerated respect for a weapon to induce complacency about its actual efficacy.

In the real world, even the possessor of a nuclear weapon system may be uncertain about its reliability. No specific weapon intended for use in war can ever be fully tested, for such a test would destroy the weapon. While it is possible and indeed essential to extrapolate from tests of samples, this cannot be done under fully realistic conditions. The nuclear test ban precludes atmospheric tests of warheads. Political considerations prevent the United States even conducting test firings of unarmed missiles from operational silos though the Soviet Union does so. But a deterrent force comprises a large number of weapons that need to be used, possibly at short warning, under conditions of great psychological and technological stress.

To destroy its target, a nuclear weapon and its delivery system must survive a number of hazards, falling to any of which would negate the whole process. The probability of system failure is the multiple, not the sum, of the probabilities of specific failures; the performance in each respect must therefore be very high indeed if the system is to succeed (e.g. the probability of success for a weapon of 90% reliability in each of ten respects, is $.9^9 = .35^-$, i.e. only a one in three probability of complete success).

The hurdles to be crossed by an ICBM are illustrated in the diagram. To these can be added others, some specific to other systems and some general to all. Aircraft are, for instance, vulnerable to crew fatigue, airframe or engine failure, and navigational errors, none of which are perhaps of a high order of probability, and to damage by enemy air defences, which is a major hazard. Cruise missiles may suffer degradation from many of the same sources. Submarine launched weapons are vulnerable to normal maritime hazards and to enemy ASW. SLBMs also exemplify one of the dangers facing all weapons: the possibility that the correct launch orders may not arrive. The machinery both administrative and technical for command and control has increasingly been recognised as a subject for concern and has become a possible prime target for enemy action. A similar burden falls on the electronics for target identification and location, and for assessing the effects of both one's own and the enemy's attacks.

The diagram identifies some of the hazards encountered by an ICBM and by its warheads during launch and the later stages of its trajectory, gives some indication of their relative seriousness as sources of mission failure and gives an impression of their cumulative effect on a salvo. Such hazards can be countered either by improving technical performance or multiplying missiles. Both are expensive, but the first is clearly preferable on strategic grounds, especially where commanders, as in limited nuclear operations, would want to have a precise notion of what the effect of a strike would actually be. Multiplication as an answer to unreliability can also send confusing messages to a foe who does not have the reliability data himself.

	target reached
	warhead malfunctions and so fails to detonate EXTREMELY LOW
	warhead misses target as a result of errors in the targeting programme VERY LOW
	anomalous conditions destroy warhead during re-entry UNPREDICTED
	damage to warhead from close-in nuclear explosion causes burn-up during re-entry UNPREDICTED
	failure in warhead dispensing sequencer VERY LOW
	failure in warhead bus control rockets VERY LOW
	failure in upper-stage rocket VERY LOW
	failure in inertial navigation system EXTREMELY LOW
	missile encounters storm and is heavily damaged UNPREDICTED
	failure to stage correctly VERY LOW
	failure in launch sequence VERY LOW
	silo door fails to open EXTREMELY LOW

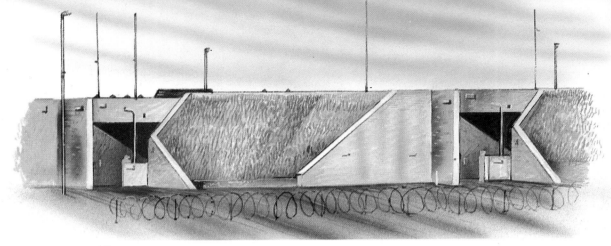

Nuclear Storage

As active defence against attack by nuclear weapons is very difficult, one of the few effective methods of defending oneself is by pre-emptive attack on the enemy weapons. This is the dominant characteristic of the strategic nuclear forces: the utmost effort to achieve "survivability". This may mean the dispersal and hiding of weapons. Where tactical and theatre forces are concerned the number of warheads involved may be very high: there are some 5000 American warheads in Western Europe. Widespread dispersal would raise many political, strategic and technical problems; local populations do not take kindly to the omnipresence of nuclear weapons, possibly dangerous in themselves and probable targets of enemy action in war. Dispersal also complicates the important task of maintaining effective, centralised political and military control.

The typical solution is to place warheads in a limited number of secure storage sites, with a capability for rapid dispersal to delivery systems and units in crisis. American weapons in Europe are centred upon some 75 sites. This policy obviously has disadvantages. The sites are high value targets, the location of which is inevitably known to the enemy. It has long been appreciated that a very simple Soviet nuclear strike could eliminate the bulk of American weapons if they were not dispersed in time; yet dispersal would be a highly conspicuous and dramatic signal that governments might be very reluctant to take. In recent years this problem has been greatly exacerbated by the probability that modern precision guided weapons could destroy the storage sites with conventional warheads. The typical site is not very "hard", is conspicuous and usually has rectangular entry doors set in an igloo-like mound that offers target-seeking devices an ideally sharp contrast to home in on. Thus the possibility arises of eliminating a great deal of an enemy's escalatory capability without oneself crossing the nuclear threshold; the potential victim may be inhibited from dispersal by fear that it will itself be read as the moment of nuclear escalation.

Modern weaponry also increases the possibility of successful sabotage of storage sites. The Soviet Union trains large numbers of "Spetznaz" forces for this role and has numerous agents in place. Elimination of nuclear weapon stores is a declared role for such forces, just as air and missile strikes for this purpose enjoy regular priority of place in Soviet discussion of targeting in the initial stages of war.

Nuclear storage sites combine hardened accommodation for weapons with provision for rapid access when dispersal is necessary, and elaborate electronic and manned security systems, including armed guards with orders to do whatever is necessary to safeguard their weapons.

To guard against such possibilities, to maintain security against terrorists, and to prevent unauthorised use of nuclear weapons absorbs a great deal of manpower. Estimates suggest the equivalent of a large US Army division as well as numerous allied forces are devoted to "custodial duties".

For all these reasons, serious consideration is being given to better methods of storage, ranging from safer sites requiring less manpower, to alternative concepts of deployment and dispersal. An extreme form would be withdrawal of all American warheads to the United States to be airlifted back in crisis. This, however, would raise practical and symbolic problems. Practically, a great deal could go wrong in crisis or war with redeployment plans. Moreover all the inhibitions making dispersal from sites difficult would attend a decision to redeploy weapons from the United States to Europe; possibly more so. For all these reasons, retirement of all weapons to the United States would probably seem a major disengagement of American nuclear power from Europe. The presence of the weapons symbolises this commitment to European defence and compels the Soviet Union to ponder the dangers of attacking or overrunning them. It is an altogether different question to debate a further sharp reduction in the number of nuclear weapons. While there are many reasons why that may be desirable, the storage problem is undoubtedly a major incentive to seek such reductions.

The Chronology of Nuclear Strategy

The world of strategy is moulded by the interaction of many factors: some of the more important are technology, strategic thought, and politics both international, between allies and adversaries, and domestic, between parties but often more importantly, between rival armed services. Some of the milestones and interactions in the nuclear age are outlined on the historical chart overleaf.

One of the most difficult relationships to analyse is that between policy and technology. In many cases it is clearly the autonomous progress of technology that drives strategy; the military simply cannot afford to neglect a possibility that technology throws up for fear that an enemy will exploit it. The most clear-cut example of this is the atom bomb itself, made possible by fundamental scientific research and brought to the attention of political leaders who had no idea of the science, and still less of its military applications. Yet sometimes politics does cut off military programmes; thus the United States was precluded from developing and deploying an enhanced radiation weapon.

Another often obscure area is the relationship between "declaratory" doctrine and what military forces are actually expecting and preparing to do. Thus recently declassified sources have made it clear that to a large extent the American Strategic Air Command was steadily increasing its capacity to execute a consistently developed plan to strike at Soviet forces and war-making potential throughout years in which American strategic doctrine seemed to be undergoing a sequence of quite significant changes. Similarly there were certainly many years during which NATO forces were trained to expect a kind of theatre nuclear war about which political leaders were increasingly sceptical.

American nuclear policy has always been dominated by the need to defend Europe (and Japan, a less difficult problem for geographical reasons) as well as preclude nuclear attack (the only form of plausible attack on the United States itself for most of the post war years) on itself. The original response to Soviet acquisition of nuclear weapons was to prepare to defend Europe conventionally. Expense and over-confidence in nuclear weapons as a panacea drove declaratory doctrine into Massive Retaliation; later scepticism about this in the face of growing Soviet power produced the flexible response and that, coupled with alleged American betrayal in the Suez crisis, drove de Gaulle out of NATO and into national nuclear independence. Later nervousness on all sides about the credibility of even the strategic action called for as the apex of flexible response produced interest in limited strategic war, for which the technology, chiefly accuracy and better C^3I, seemed available.

Meanwhile there had been complicated interaction at the technological level. Fears of vulnerability of American forces, exacerbated by the erroneous belief bred by Sputnik that the Soviet Union was far ahead in missile technology, accelerated development and deployment of silo and submarine based missiles. Later still multiple warheads, a way of increasing the effectiveness of depleted offensive forces, became both a possible answer to early ABM defences and a counterforce threat to fixed land-based missiles. From that threat emerged, in part, new mobile missiles, more accurate SLBMs, and cruise missiles.

The Soviet Union seems to have worried less about vulnerability, at least in the past. It was late to adopt silo-basing and to perfect SLBMs; it still keeps less of its forces on alert. The reason for this is obscure but important; does it stem from a lack of capability or, perhaps, from an intention to strike first? At the outset of the nuclear age the Soviet Union minimised the importance of nuclear weapons; this was natural in a power without this form of weapon but Stalin probably also believed the doctrine of "permanently operating factors": in essence the belief that surprise and the early stages of war could not offset war potential. The Soviet Union still stresses more than the Western powers that nuclear weapons are embedded in the total matrix of military and political power.

After Stalin, however, Soviet military writers began to stress the decisive role of nuclear weapons in the early stages of war. Krushchev at first tried to use this idea to economise on military forces while extracting political gains, notably in Berlin, from the exaggerated reputation of Soviet nuclear power. Thwarted in Berlin and in his effort at a quick fix by placing nuclear weapons in Cuba, Krushchev began the process accelerated under Brezhnev of building up Soviet military power at all levels. One feature of this effort was that Soviet intermediate and medium range weapons threatening Western Europe, once an adjunct to weak intercontinental power holding Europe as a "hostage" to American behaviour, were now refurbished with the purpose of creating a separate threat to NATO "decoupled" from the direct Superpower stand-off.

STRATEGIC HISTORY

TIME	WEAPONS
Late 1940s	B29 A-bomb B36
1952	H-bomb-B47
1953	
	Thor, Jupiter IRBM
1956+	B52
1960+	Polaris A1 SLBM Titan 2
1962	Minuteman I, Minuteman II Silos
1964	
1966	FB III
1970+	Minuteman III Poseidon SLBM MIRV/ABM
1974	
1979	Trident 1 Cruise
1980	Minuteman 3 with 12A MIRV
1983	Ohio SSBN
1985	Midgetman mobile ICBM development
1986	MX/B1

U.S. DOCTRINE	EVENTS	S.U. DOCTRINE	WEAPONS
rld War II + A-bomb errence by Defence	Berlin Blockade 1948-9 North Atlantic Treaty Korean War 1950	World War II again – "permanently operating factors"	Conventional Red Army + 1949 = A-bomb test
oss the Board Defence ventional Rearmament bon" Force Goals		World War II + atomic	
assive Retaliation" errence by "punishment"	Death of Stalin 1953 NATO adopts nuclear weapon use '54 U.K. A-bomb		'52-'55 Soviet H-bomb Badger
lic critique of Massive Retaliation trines of Limited War	Khruschev '56+; Suez '56; Sputnik 1957; France goes for A-bomb Berlin crisis '58–; Quemoy-Matsu crisis de Gaulle in power '58 Soviet/Chinese split JF Kennedy President '60 Berlin Wall '61	War no longer inevitable under Leninism – Nuclear Emphasis Bluff based on supposed power	SS4-5 IRBM. Bear
xible Response" advocated for NATO	Cuban Missile Crisis '62 Nuclear Testban '63		
nage Limitation by controlled nterforce (McNamara) tual) Assured Destruction: Stable nce given by invulnerable technology	Brezhnev '64 Chinese nuclear weapons '64	Build real nuclear strength to Parity – nuclear war can be fought and won	SS7-8 ICBM Blinder
fficiency" – more than minimal errence – Stability from arms control	De Gaulle leaves NATO '66 NATO adopts "Flexible Response" '67 NATO Nuclear Planning Group 1969	Increase naval power – overseas operations Improve Theatre Nuclear Forces	SS9-11 Galosh ABM Yankee SSBN Delta SSBN
ited Strategic Options	'72 – SALT 1 + ABM Treaty agreed '73 Yom Kippur War = US nuclear alert	Even 'victory' in nuclear war suicidal Substantial wars even between US and Soviet Union might be non-nuclear at least at start: improve capability to conduct wholly conventional operations	Backfire MIRV – SS 17/18/19 SS20 – IRBM/MIRV Hardened command
9 – Carter endorses limited options	1979 NATO accepts dual-track decision on GLCM/Pershing II deployment. SALT II signed '79 Soviet Union invades Afghanistan '79		
ntervailing Strategy – limited -fighting' potential tegic Defense Initiative tual Assured Survival" proposal	Cruise/Pershing deployed in Europe		Typhoon SSBN SS-N-20 Blackjack SS24/25 Mobile ICBM

Command, Control, Communications an

For a nuclear force to constitute a credible deterrent and, if activated, an effective military force, it must remain under adequate command and control. It must execute the operations called for by the national commanders and, equally important where strikes may be taken as signals of intent and provoke retaliation, must not do anything unauthorised. What system of command, control and communication will be adequate varies with the nature of the force and with the strategic purpose it serves.

Centrepiece of the American command and control system for nuclear war are the National Emergency Airborne Command Posts, based upon the Boeing 747, of which four provide a hopefully ready and invulnerable facility for the President and his staff (the National Command Authority, or NCA). Dual-based at Offut in Nebraska and Andrews near Washington DC, the force has long endurance, backed up by in-flight refuelling and duplicate crews. Elaborate C^3I

Boeing E-4B advanced airborne command post

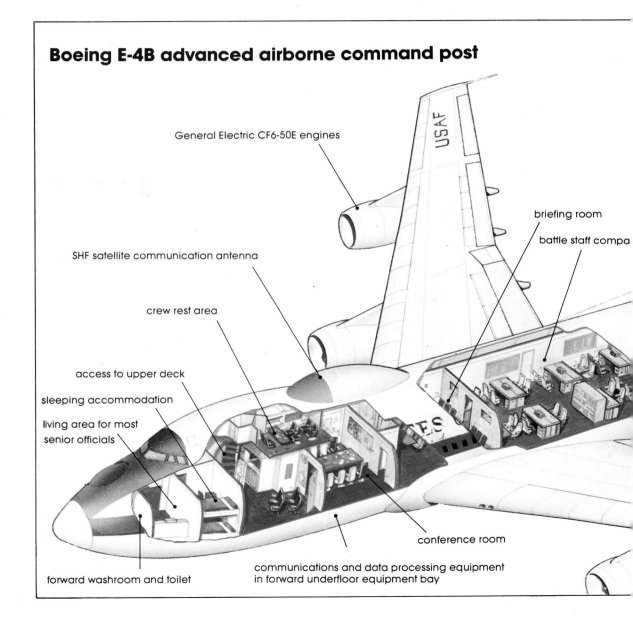

General Electric CF6-50E engines

briefing room

battle staff compa

SHF satellite communication antenna

crew rest area

access to upper deck

sleeping accommodation

living area for most senior officials

forward washroom and toilet

conference room

communications and data processing equipment in forward underfloor equipment bay

...telligence (C^3I)

...equipment links the NCA to the military command system and particularly to the nuclear forces through ground, space and other airborne links. A new Ground Wave Emergency Network (GWEN), initially in service in 1987, provides the only EMP-hardened system linking the NCA to both warning systems and the retaliatory forces.

The popular image of a nuclear war as a single spasm of mutual destruction tends to minimise both the importance and the difficulty of maintaining satisfactory C^3. If a strategy were simply one of all-out retaliation for any nuclear attack it might be suggested, for instance, that all that was necessary was to send a few SSBNs to sea with orders to fire upon a set of enemy cities if in any particular week an order not to do so was not received. A moment's reflection reveals, however, that the very simplicity of this targeting plan makes such a crude system of control

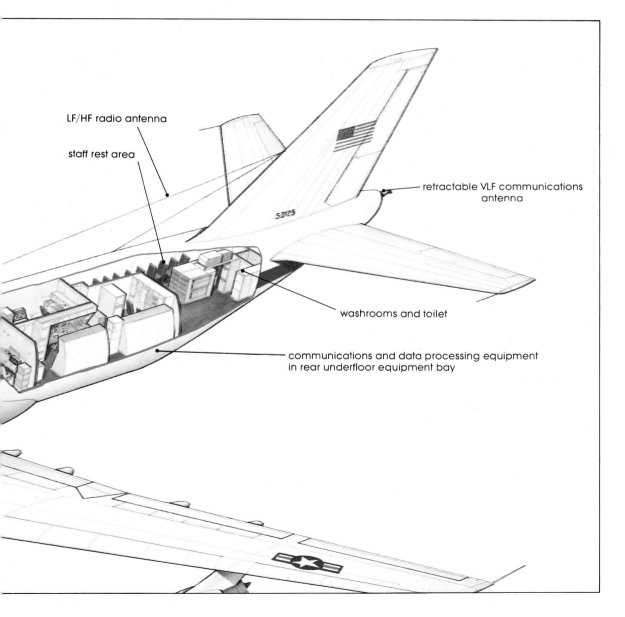

LF/HF radio antenna

staff rest area

retractable VLF communications antenna

washrooms and toilet

communications and data processing equipment in rear underfloor equipment bay

unacceptable; for if some failure led a submarine commander to fire when this was not intended by the national commanders, the nature of his strike would be one of the most likely to prompt a devastating response. Once one sets higher standards of information and of authorisation or establishes more limited, precise, and therefore probably less dangerous targeting, the specifications for C^3I become immensely more demanding.

Ideally an adequate C^3I system should provide the commanders with timely warning of attack. It should be able to assess damage and the current readiness of friendly forces, to update information on enemy forces and targets, contribute to choosing the best course of action, select the optimal military operations, issue the necessary orders, assess the results and be prepared to repeat the whole cycle. Whether the system can do all this will depend on the investment made and the operations conducted by the enemy. Against a powerful foe, the system will undoubtedly degrade; again ideally it should do so "gracefully", keeping the most essential capabilities until last. Among these may well be a capacity to communicate with the enemy himself.

The problems of C^3I were first fully appreciated, at least in the United States, in the mid-1950s. At that time much theoretical and practical work was done to make C^3I systems sufficiently robust to give assurance of a "secure second strike" and to prevent unauthorised use of weapons, whether in a military fashion or for terrorist purposes. For the latter function two-key systems were devised to see that more than one authorised operator was necessary to launch a weapon — a procedure particularly significant where, as in NATO, American weapons are to be used by other nations — and later electronic digital switches (PAL – Permissive Action Links) were installed on many weapons so that higher command could quickly pass release codes not previously known to the end-user of the weapon.

By the standards that are now demanded of C^3I in a climate where the controlled and limited use of nuclear weapons appears more desirable, if use there must be, than full-scale first or retaliatory strikes, the steps taken in previous decades seem inadequate. Nevertheless, both the Soviet Union and the United States have devoted considerable effort to C^3I and the lesser nuclear powers have attempted to do somewhat the same, though their strategies have usually been less demanding.

C^3I can be protected by a variety of means of which the chief are the hardening of facilities against an attack, mobility and concealment, and redundancy. The Soviet Union has long devoted strenuous efforts to such measures and undertook extensive hardening and other modes of protection to C^3I well before it invested in similar protection for the weapons themselves. Perhaps the most well-known provision for C^3I are the E4 and other aircraft designed to keep the President of the United States alive and in contact with his forces. The basic warning network for North America is centred upon the North American Air Defence Command (NORAD), a joint US-Canadian facility under Cheyenne Mountain near Colorado Springs; this base, originally invulnerable, is now probably not so, particularly in respect of communications.

The Soviet Union is also well-known to pay particular attention to counter-C^3I capability; that is, the ability to degrade and destroy enemy

The United States currently places high priority on strengthening communica[tions] between sensors, commanders and weapons. A major element in the programme is the concept of redunda[ncy] both within and between sub-system[s so] the degradation of the system is gradu[al] preserving the most essential functio[ns to] the end. Another element is mobility [on] land, in the air and in space. The pictu[re]

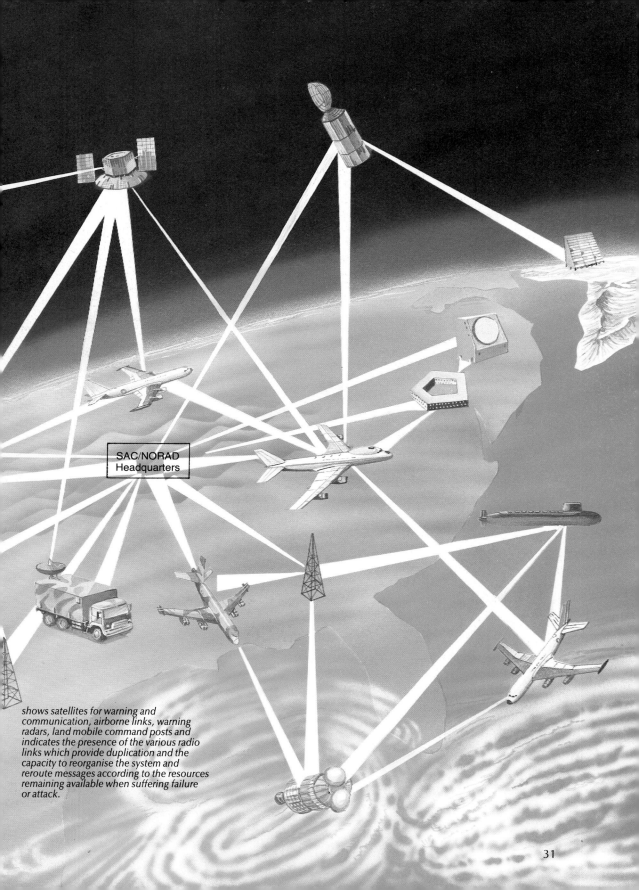

SAC/NORAD
Headquarters

shows satellites for warning and
communication, airborne links, warning
radars, land mobile command posts and
indicates the presence of the various radio
links which provide duplication and the
capacity to reorganise the system and
reroute messages according to the resources
remaining available when suffering failure
or attack.

C³I and thus to render his forces ineffective. Clearly counter-C³I operations can be devastating to an enemy's war fighting capability but they need to be approached carefully, for while it may be wholly advantageous to remove your enemy's capacity to hurt you, you do not want, particularly where nuclear weapons are concerned, to destroy his capacity to restrain himself. Thus the value of counter-C³I operations and the best way if any of executing them is very dependent on what the strategies and the C³I systems of the combatants are.

The weight of expenditure on C³I within military budgets is rising rapidly for all forms of combat. Where nuclear weapons are involved, the current interest in more limited operations is paralleled by, and indeed to a great extent made possible by, the lightening pace of electronics. The combination of escalating capability for computing and communicating at relatively if not absolutely lower and lower cost is making hitherto unthinkable performance possible. Vulnerability of electronics to the electromagnetic pulse emitted by nuclear explosions constitutes a serious problem; to this optical fibre offers a solution in some applications. The components of communication systems are also vulnerable to other forms of damage. Some of the most revolutionary capabilities are offered by satellites — unrivalled in reconnaissance — but these are themselves now vulnerable to attack. Some believe the Soviet preference for smaller, lower orbit, expendable satellites in large numbers provides a system less vulnerable as a whole, and that the capability for frequent launches required for such a practice provides an ability to "surge" a network and to regenerate it during warfare that the United States currently lacks. On the other hand, the components of the American systems are almost certainly more effective in themselves.

Among the most significant contributions to the security and survivability of communications is the digitalisation of information. This is permitting the "packet-switching" of messages. In this concept, already in use in civilian and military systems, messages are broken into components each of which also carries information about source and destination. This enables a network automatically to route messages by the most effective path and reconstitute them when received. In doing this, the network informs itself of its own state and performance so that gaps in the system arising from failure or damage can be bypassed, permitting a high degree of surviving capacity without excessive redundancy.

Particular difficulty attends communication with submerged submarines because radio waves do not readily penetrate water — a phenomenon that contributes substantially to the invulnerability of submarines. In the past and at present SSBNs can receive messages only by approaching the surface with a trailed antenna, a constraint mitigated by use of very low (VLF) or extremely low (ELF) frequencies. The latter, however, require immense vulnerable land based transmitting antennae and have very low transmission rates. A major system for communication with submarines, designated TACAMO (Take Command and Move Out), employs long trailing antennae mounted on EC 130 Hercules aircraft, to be replaced in the 'nineties by modified Boeing 707 (E6).

1 An E-4B AABNCP communications aircraft leaves Washington with the President on board.

5 SS-19 ICBM's destroy NORAD's Cheyenne headquarters.

2 NORAD headquarters under Cheyenne mountain monitors the Soviet attack.

3 Satellites keep NORAD, the President and other command centres fully in touch.

4 Aboard the E-4B incoming data is processed and acted upon.

6 In ground-located headquarters, attacks by US missile submarines are ordered and controlled.

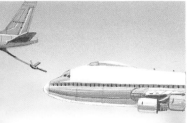

7 The President's E-4B is kept airborne by inflight-refuelling.

8 If the conflict ends after a limited exchange the E-4B lands at a remote airfield.

Limited Strategic War

When the United States first acquired atomic weapons they were scarce and expected to remain so; at the same time the only delivery system, piston-engined bombers, were vulnerable to air defences. As a result nuclear weapons first appeared to be a useful but perhaps not decisive supplement to the kind of strategic bombing used in the previous World War. One deleterious effect of the new bombs on strategic thought was, however, to make precise targeting of vital facilities — one of the great conceptual and technological achievements of World War II — seem less important, with a consequent drift to regarding cities themselves as targets. The advent of "nuclear plenty", in the early 1950s and of the H-bomb, led to the adoption of city bombing as a preferred strategy and deterrence of all aggression was expected to derive from a generalised threat against cities and population. At the same time the USAF still maintained traditional military concepts of targeting and kept the retardation (ROMEO) and blunting (BRAVO) targets on the list. The BRAVO targets were at first chiefly Soviet air bases and the large number of these drove up the Strategic Air Command (SAC) force requirements: by 1956 SAC had identified almost 3,000 targets. While most of these were "military", particularly air bases, the strike implied would have been indistinguishable from a deliberate "city busting" assault.

Massive Retaliation was soon criticised for incredibility because, with Soviet forces growing, it implied a massive Soviet strike on the United States which would hardly be a sound price for Americans to pay to halt lesser Soviet aggressions. John F. Kennedy campaigned on the message that not only had US strategic forces become inferior — which was wrong — but that the strategy meant "Holocaust or Humiliation".

Under Kennedy as President there began an uncertain progress toward more limited strategies. In 1962 his Secretary of Defense, Robert McNamara, announced a policy of counterforce targeting and city sparing to reduce the damage done to the United States in two ways — by weakening Soviet forces and giving them an incentive to moderation by retaining their (undamaged) cities as "hostages". Although the multiplication of US nuclear forces and the entry of a new service, the US Navy, into the strategic nuclear business, had impelled the formation in 1960 of the first Single Integrated Operational Plan (SIOP), this was not differentiated into separable packages and certainly not any of a significantly limited nature. Partly to curb SAC demands, McNamara switched his overt doctrine to Assured Destruction: the belief that a limited capability could do devastating "unacceptable damage" to the Soviet Union and hence deter a Soviet nuclear attack. Tactical nuclear weapons and conventional forces would have to deal at least with the initial stages of lesser aggressions by way of a "flexible response".

By the late 1960s this strategy also looked threadbare. It offered no escape from permanent vulnerability to annihilation if deterrence once failed, and nothing to hope for once war began. Moreover it failed to describe or to control the actual much more traditionally strategic targeting policy of the USAF/USN SIOP aimed in large part at Soviet war-making potential. Furthermore, the Soviet Union itself had never

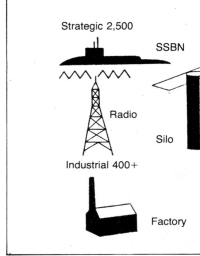

Strategic 2,500

SSBN

Radio

Silo

Industrial 400+

Factory

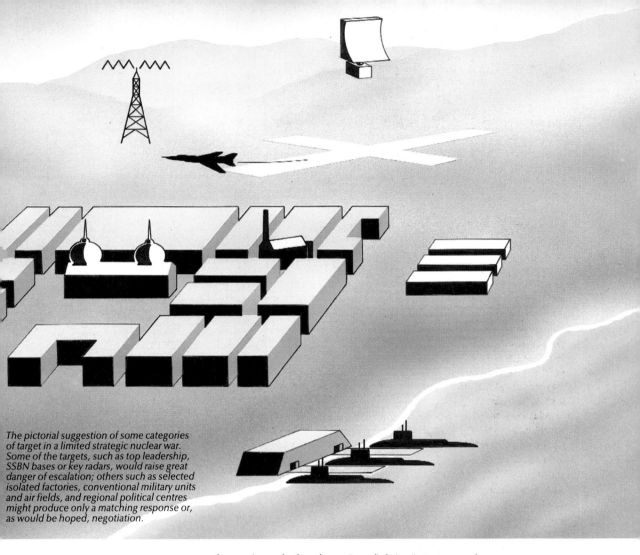

The pictorial suggestion of some categories of target in a limited strategic nuclear war. Some of the targets, such as top leadership, SSBN bases or key radars, would raise great danger of escalation; others such as selected isolated factories, conventional military units and air fields, and regional political centres might produce only a matching response or, as would be hoped, negotiation.

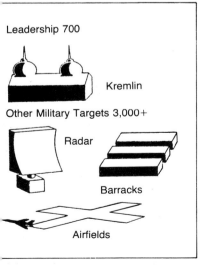

Leadership 700

Kremlin

Other Military Targets 3,000+

Radar

Barracks

Airfields

shown signs of other than a "war fighting" strategy and was consequently thought by many to be able to retain hopes of meaningful "victory" inconceivable within a doctrine of assured destruction. This raised fears that the Soviet Union might have an important psychological advantage in crisis and also a reason to fire first in an extreme crisis because of hopes of pre-empting an American attack that, if launched, would spare nothing and thus leave nothing to lose by going first.

Such considerations aroused fears of paralysis in crisis, especially as the flexible response doctrine in NATO called for the United States to be ready to initiate the use of nuclear weapons if the earlier lines of defence failed. This fear was summed up by President Nixon in 1971 when he declared:

> *"I must not be and my successors must not be limited to the indiscriminate mass destruction of enemy civilians as the sole possible response to challenges. This is expecially so when that response involves the likelihood of triggering nuclear attacks on our own population."*

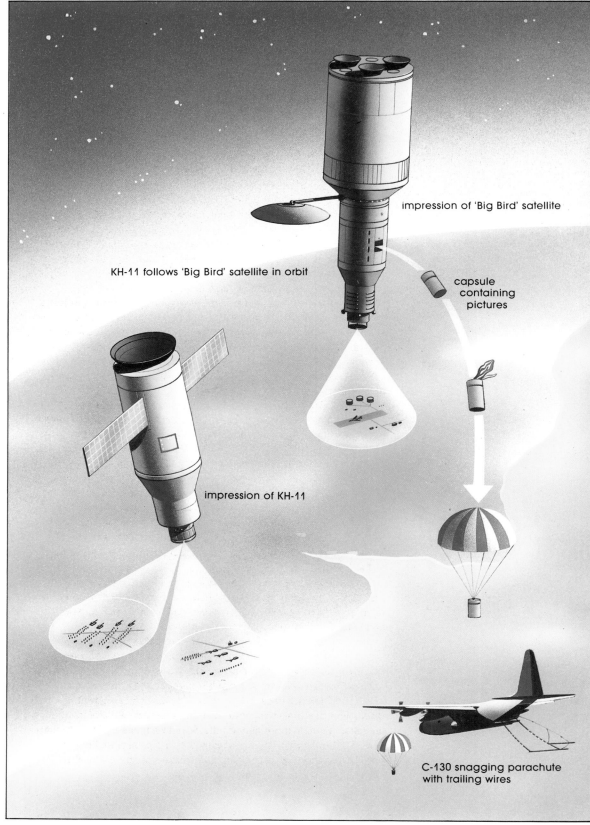

impression of 'Big Bird' satellite

KH-11 follows 'Big Bird' satellite in orbit

capsule containing pictures

impression of KH-11

C-130 snagging parachute with trailing wires

The answer was to revive ideas that first made a tentative appearance in the mid 1950s; that even strategic nuclear weapons might be used in limited ways, leaving such ultimate targets as cities unscathed and consequently hostages to ensure the equal restraint of the enemy. Beginning in 1974 under James Schlesinger as Secretary of Defense and later confirmed under President Carter in a famous Presidential Directive (PD) 59, efforts were made to devise more discriminatory target plans. Gradually there has been a progress from merely trying to isolate subsets of existing target plans to drawing up plans in which limitation and minimisation of casualties are prime criteria. There have also been increased efforts to provide forces and control mechanisms capable of executing such limited strikes. These efforts have been facilitated by new C^3 capabilities and greatly increased accuracy, permitting the "micro-targeting" of specific objectives and hence the assignment of much smaller warheads. Accuracy is now such that even conventional warheads may be able to destroy targets once thought only vulnerable to nuclear explosions.

Many questions and doubts surround this trend in American strategy. By making nuclear war seem less catastrophic, necessary if it is to appear a usable option in, for example, the extension of nuclear guarantees ("extended deterrence") to allies, will a strategy of limited nuclear war make such a war more likely? Advocates argue that plenty of deterrent, caution-inducing terror will remain, and that it must surely be wise to have some ways of trying to limit the consequences if deterrence fails.

Other doubters question whether nuclear weapons can be used without catastrophic consequences. These doubts tend to be reinforced by a few well-publicised studies in which the so-called "limited" strikes are not really very limited, e.g. some 100 MT expended on an ICBM force. Even so, terrible though casualties of the order of 10 million would be, the result is significantly different from the 100 million or so envisaged in classical scenarios for assured destruction campaigns between Superpowers. Truly limited attacks on military targets, accepting the avoidance of those where high collateral damage seems inevitable, can at least in theory tightly confine casualties and longer term consequences; the latter mainly by eschewing fall-out producing ground bursts.

Another doubt concerns Soviet willingness to adopt equally restrained tactics. Because limited nuclear operations might resolve the dilemma of NATO and the United States in trying to use US nuclear power to bolster European defence, the Soviet Union has loudly denounced limited nuclear options as impracticable and immoral, warning that any nuclear war would inevitably escalate out of control. But Soviet doctrine has never made a virtue of destruction for its own sake and obviously if a nuclear war began the Soviet Union would have a keen vested interest in curbing its effects. In recent years Soviet discussions of war have suggested a more favourable attitude to limitation. Perhaps more significantly, Soviet weapons and the attention paid to C^3I and to civil defence suggest a high capability for limited nuclear operations, if that is what Soviet leaders opt for if and when war comes.

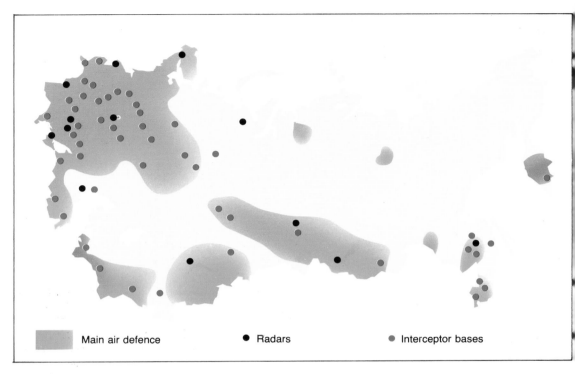

Main air defence   ● Radars   ● Interceptor bases

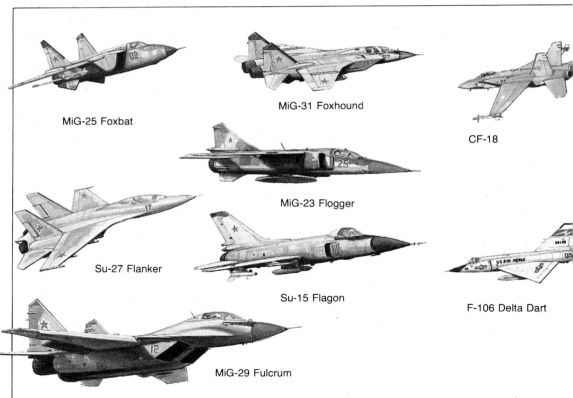

MiG-25 Foxbat

MiG-31 Foxhound

CF-18

MiG-23 Flogger

Su-27 Flanker

Su-15 Flagon

F-106 Delta Dart

MiG-29 Fulcrum

The Soviet Union has consistently maintained heavy air defences. The map shows major interceptor bases (blue), major radars (black) and denser areas of anti-aircraft missile deployment (shaded areas).

Air Defence

The task of defence against air attack naturally dates back to World War I when the first bombing aircraft stimulated the appearance of anti-aircraft guns and interceptor aircraft. During the inter-war years the improvement of bomber aircraft led many to believe it would enjoy terrifying ascendancy in a future war. The Italian General Douhet expounded a famous theory of victory achieved entirely through airpower, a British Prime Minister was reputed to assert that "the bomber will always get through" and the German and Italian air forces gave impressive though misleading demonstrations during the Spanish Civil War.

In the event the defence did better than expected during World War II. The most important factor in this was the invention of radar as the basis for integrated systems of fighter control. By the latter stages of the war Allied bombers achieved ascendancy in German air space and American aircraft did likewise over Japan.

These were, however, exhausted nations facing overwhelming odds. Bomber forces were still very vulnerable and because of the limitations of conventional bombs, requiring repeated missions, attrition rates of even a few per cent per mission could be unacceptable. Nuclear weapons reversed the picture. Once thermonuclear warheads became relatively plentiful even penetration rates of a few per cent became unacceptable to a defence, at least if the targets were vulnerable cities.

Despite these unfavourable odds, air defence became a major concern in the early nuclear years when aircraft were virtually the only delivery system. Soviet concentration on missiles later led the United States to neglect the air defence of the United States itself, while the strength of the USAF preserved air defence as a major Soviet priority. The Soviet Union is also vulnerable to aircraft involved in a European theatre war; for the same reason NATO Europe has developed a sophisticated missile and interceptor defence, the most fully integrated part of NATO because of the need for prompt, co-ordinated response.

More recently still the appearance of the cruise missile and of improved aircraft in Soviet forces has begun a revival of US air defence. Other factors bringing revival are the rising interest in limited nuclear operations, against which defence may be more practicable, and at least in theatre warfare the possibility that in order to control escalation attackers may try to execute formerly nuclear missions with conventional means. Thus the increased range and improved performance of Soviet ground attack aircraft have compelled the United Kingdom to take emergency steps to reinforce its neglected air defences and to invest heavily in the interceptor version of the Tornado.

Yet another stimulus to air defence is the renewed interest in ABM defence. If that is to prove useful the defender must deny the attacker an easy answer by recourse to aerodynamic vehicles. Thus ABM defences and air defences are complementary. Indeed some of the technology both for warning and interception is relevant to both threats.

As always a dialectic has developed between these air defence programmes and the techniques for penetrating defences with aircraft

Below, flying from the left are the chief current Soviet strategic defence aircraft of which some 1250 are in service together with about 1000 similar aircraft in the Tactical Air Forces. The US (on the right) operates only about 300 interceptors in the strategic role, some obsolescent, but is modernising with F 15 and F 16. Canada operates 36 F 18 interceptors.

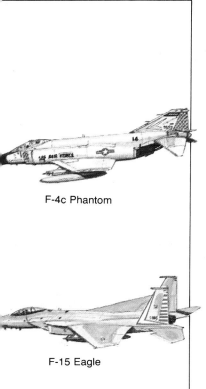

F-4c Phantom

F-15 Eagle

and cruise missiles. Low flying profile missions, electronic countermeasures to jam and evade detecting devices, other electronic measures to confuse anti-aircraft weapons and flares to distract heat seeking missiles, together with defence suppression missiles that home on defensive radars are all well-established in the offensive inventory. Today the greatest excitement surrounds so-called "stealth" technology, intended to make aircraft virtually invisible to detection. Detection of the attacking aircraft for warning, tracking them for interception, and guiding interceptor weapons to their targets are obviously indispensable for a defence. Stealth involves the exploitation of many technologies to thwart the defences in these respects. Among the devices are design of the aircraft itself to produce a smooth shape giving poor reflection to radar and other sensors, use of radar absorbent materials and paints and adoption of many active and passive electronic measures to evade or deceive radar and other detection devices. Many of these measures can be adapted in part to cheaper improvements to delivery vehicles than the full and costly stealth treatment. Some enthusiasts predict the rapid obsolescence over the next decade of any aircraft or cruise missile without a generous measure of stealth technology.

The B2 Advanced Technology Bomber (ATB) is the much discussed but still very secret in detail "Stealth" aircraft due to enter service in the early 1990s. Although highly classified, the design is believed to exploit a flying wing shape with engines concealed within the wing to reduce both radar and infra-red images. Active and passive devices and materials further reduce the "signature" of the aircraft.

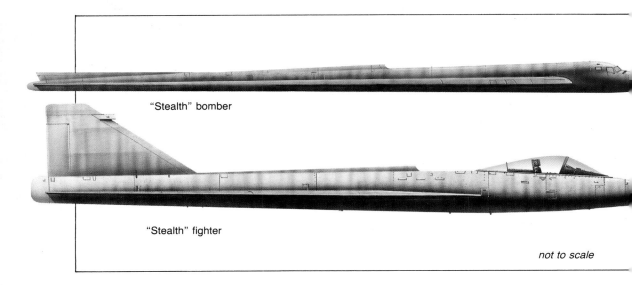

"Stealth" bomber

"Stealth" fighter

not to scale

Even less is known of the stealth fighter. Indeed its existence is largely based on speculation, unlike the ATB which was revealed by President Carter in 1980. Secret orders are said to have been placed for over 100 aircraft and the USAF has announced formation of six additional reconnaissance/strike squadrons for which the stealth fighter may be destined. If deployed, a tactical stealth aircraft might be used for very difficult penetration missions including suppression of air defences to help other more conventional aircraft in later waves.

"Stealth" fighter

Layered Strategic Defence

The fundamental elements giving new hope to proponents of strategic anti-missile defence are new methods of missile detection and kill coupled with the concept of a layered defence in which the attack suffers successive attritions. The three main layers in a defence would be boost-phase, mid-course and terminal re-entry interception. According to most experts, terminal defences are closest to useful deployment; some believe boost-phase interception could be practicable as early as 1992. The mid-course phase is least advanced. On its own, terminal defence would be most useful for "point defence" of high value military targets, both because these are usually harder and because the coverage (or "footprint") of a terminal defence is inevitably more restricted than mid-course defence. Boost-phase interception is, of course, relevant to any target accessible to the offence; indeed one advantage of such interception is that the attacker cannot know which part of his force will suffer attrition and so cannot concentrate his fire on the more heavily defended areas. This would be a major element in one of the more valuable contributions of strategic defence to deterrence:

The large diagram sketches components of a boost phase defence showing surveillance and tracking satellites, a ground-based laser using space-borne mirrors and a kinetic kill vehicle launcher. Boost to cruising speed takes some four to five minutes. In this case a particle beam detector satellite takes observations to aid the defence. An effective boost defence would greatly reduce the advantages of MIRV and of decoys because neither would reach dispersal.

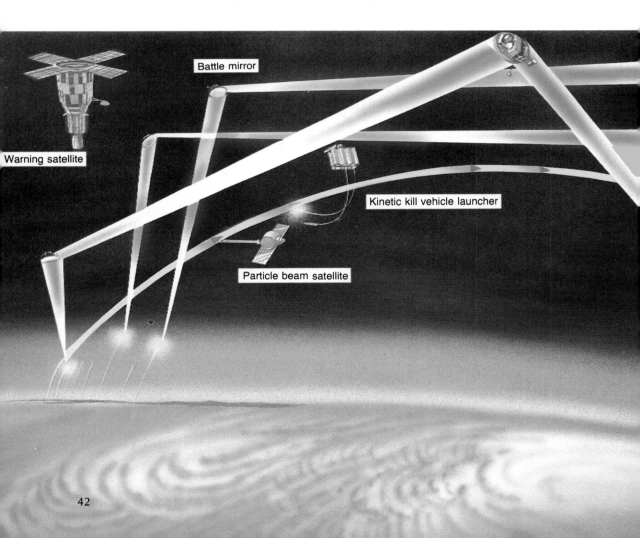

Battle mirror

Warning satellite

Kinetic kill vehicle launcher

Particle beam satellite

The small diagram shows a terminal defence here defending ICBM silos. Re-entry vehicles begin to decelerate in the atmosphere and betray different characteristics from simple decoys at about 96-112 km (60-70 miles) altitude. In this case satellite, airborne and ground-based phased array radars acquire, discriminate and track targets. Silo or mobile-based high acceleration interceptors rise to kill re-entry vehicles in some two minutes. The kill mechanisms are probably non-nuclear — conventional explosive or kinetic projectiles. Terminal defence can be effective alone, catch "leakers" from earlier phases of defence, and is the only way to deal with depressed trajectory SLBMs or IRBMs.

reducing the attacker's confidence in the outcome of his assault.

A defence would use ground, air and satellite-based sensors to detect launch and track offensive weapons. A terminal defence would rely for kill in the near future on interceptor missiles; later, ground-based lasers might be adopted. Boost-phase defence is a prime candidate for the use of lasers as the targets are soft and multiple, making repeat fire useful. However, the problem of getting the necessary laser energy into space, whether on board satellites or by way of satellite-borne mirror deflection, is far from solved and some believe it insoluble in principle. The most advocated mechanism for boost-phase interception in the near future is satellite-borne "kinetic kill vehicles (KKV)": small inert rockets. A proposed scheme for the early 1990s would use four surveillance satellites, 10 tracking satellites and a KKV force of from 500-1500 small satellites, at a suggested cost of $120 billion; others put the cost of effective defences at a trillion dollars even if practicable.

The offence has numerous possible countermeasures available, including decoys, chaff, hardening of re-entry vehicles, faster boost, attacks on satellites, and precursor nuclear bursts to blind the defence with EMP and heat. There are also many non-ballistic delivery systems.

Relay mirror

Ground based lazers

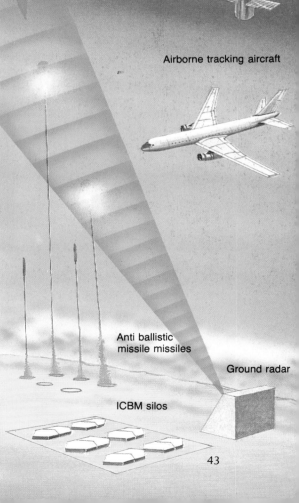

Airborne tracking aircraft

Anti ballistic missile missiles

Ground radar

ICBM silos

43

ABM

Interest in anti-ballistic missile defences was greatly increased and research and development entered a decisive new phase in March 1983 when President Reagan initiated an *"effort to define a long term research and development program . . . to achieve our ultimate goal of eliminating the threat posed by strategic nuclear missiles."* By setting this goal the President questioned one of the basic assumptions of the accepted nuclear strategy: that there could be no effective defence against ballistic missiles. He also virtually repudiated the concept of nuclear deterrence itself, for strategic stability was widely believed to rest most firmly precisely on mutual vulnerability with the ballistic missile the most powerful instrument to achieve this.

All weapons tend to set up a dialectic relationship with countermeasures and it was only to be expected that, as soon as operational ballistic missiles appeared, intense thought was given to intercepting them in flight. The task is, however, a formidable one and long proved technologically daunting. Both the Soviet Union and the United States had active development programmes in the 1950s, and in the mid-1960s the Soviet Union began deployment of a system on interceptor missiles code-named Galosh around Moscow. A few years previously the United States had decided not to deploy a somewhat similar system on the grounds that while it was possible to intercept individual warheads in tests, in practice the task of penetrating such a defence would prove much cheaper than that of reinforcing the defence.

By the mid-1960s several technological advances made the prospects brighter. One advance concerned radars which, coupled to rapidly improving computers, made it more practicable to detect and track incoming warheads and to guide interceptor missiles towards them. Another advance stemmed from the realisation that nuclear interceptor warheads would generate X-rays on explosion that would travel far in space — where there was no atmosphere to impede them — and damage incoming warheads and especially their electrical systems over a wide area, thereby reducing the need for accurate interception.

A third advance related to "decoys". One easy measure to deceive a defence is for an offensive missile to release several light, cheap simulations of a real warhead which are indistinguishable from a real warhead in space where the difference in weight does not affect trajectory. Once in the atmosphere, however, the light decoys are easily distinguished. By developing interceptor missiles with very high acceleration, it was found possible to wait to this late stage and still intercept, even though large nuclear defensive warheads could not be used so low over soft targets.

As a result of these developments the United States began to deploy an Anti-Ballistic Missile (ABM) system in the mid-1960s. At first this was a "thin" defence for the whole United States of America, called Sentinel; later difficulties prompted concentration upon defending Washington DC as the national command centre and the fields of US offensive ICBMs. This system was named Safeguard.

While all this was going on, a heated strategic debate proceeded in the United States, in the NATO alliance and even between the United

An artist's very generalised impression of some "Starwars" approaches to anti-missile defence depicts ground-based laser interception, space-based laser attack on missiles in early and late boost stages of both ICBM and SLBM, and anti-satellite hunter killers approaching target-acquiring components of the ABM force.

States and Soviet spokesmen as to the strategic and political effects and desirability of ABM. Those who saw strategic stability as best based on mutual vulnerability feared ABM would set off an offence-defence arms race of the traditional kind. Those who were sceptical about the technology and economics of ABM also believed the defence would always lose and that the race would be pointless. They therefore advocated an arms control agreement to limit or ban ABM. At first the Soviet Union, believing itself to be ahead in ABM and inferior in offensive missiles, argued that there could in principle be nothing objectionable about weapons that were defensive and saved lives. Later as they saw American technology advance and the United States begin to deploy a system, they reversed their position, while the United States, more conscious of the pace of Soviet deployment of offensive missiles, began to take a greater interest in curbs on those.

It was against this background that the ABM Treaty of 1972 limited ABM deployment to two localised systems for each country, each of 100 interceptor missiles, one around the national capital — to obviate dismantling Galosh — and one around an ICBM field, to permit the initial Safeguard deployment. The ABM Treaty also placed limits on R & D that were to arouse controversy. Parallel to the ABM Treaty was an Interim Agreement on offensive missiles, known as SALT 1.

The United States soon abandoned its Safeguard system as ineffective; the Soviet Union maintained and has steadily updated the Galosh system. Both countries continued R & D, the Soviet Union generally more vigorously than the United States, in which doctrinal doubts about the wisdom of ABM were more pronounced.

The programme President Reagan launched in 1983, the Strategic Defence Initiative (SDI), commonly known as Starwars, inaugurated not merely an expensive R & D effort but a heated new strategic debate. As in the 1960s the basic occasion was technological progress. By 1980 electronics had greatly advanced the art of detecting and tracking missiles and re-entry vehicles. Interceptor missiles could now be so accurate as to be effective without nuclear warheads; this greatly relaxed constraints on deployment and the mode of engaging targets. Satellites made it possible to consider emplacing interceptor systems in space and attacking missiles as they rose out of their silos or submarines, at which "boost stage" they are slow, vulnerable and have not yet separated their multiple warheads. While this and other forms of inter-ception could be undertaken by projectiles of one kind or another, it was by now possible to think of using lasers or other radiation weapons that would have a rapid refire capability permitting shoot-look-shoot tactics. Moreover, it was possible to apply such ideas to the difficult but the longest lasting opportunity for interception, the mid-course phase when the re-entry vehicles are cruising unpowered through space.

It is the possibility of combining interception at all these phases in a "layered" defence that offers the most promising theoretical performance; 50% effectiveness in each phase would permit only 12% of the attack to filter through.

President Reagan's decision to press ahead was stimulated in part by knowledge that Soviet R & D was active and making great strides. The Galosh system was the world's only operational ABM system. A new Soviet air defence missile, the SA12, was believed to have been tested

The diagram gives a general impression of the types of orbit employed by satellites for various purposes. Only the geostationary equatorial orbits provide steady surveillance of specific areas of the globe's surface. The optimal way of conducting particular surveillance functions evolves with the technology of satellites and sensors and with that of data transmission. Digitalised packet switched data can now enable satellites to pass information so quickly and in such quantities that that acquired by any satellite could in principle be virtually instantly available to its operators on the ground.

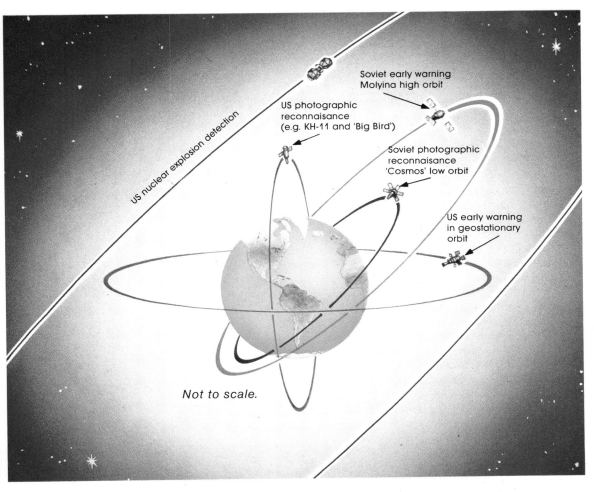

US nuclear explosion detection

US photographic reconnaisance (e.g. KH-11 and 'Big Bird')

Soviet early warning Molyina high orbit

Soviet photographic reconnaisance 'Cosmos' low orbit

US early warning in geostationary orbit

Not to scale.

and to have considerable capability as an ABM. The always elaborate Soviet air defence system provided a set of radars possibly amenable to upgrade for ABM purposes, and in alleged defiance of the ABM Treaty the Soviet Union was building a very large phased array radar at Krasnoyarsk that might constitute the one missing link in a Soviet network of battle-management facilities for a nationwide ABM system.

There still remain many issues to debate, however, as to whether ABM is effective or desirable. As always what matters is the balance of costs: can the offence break through the defence at acceptable cost? If a powerful nation believes it needs an offensive nuclear capability against a foe, it will obviously be willing to put a high price on it and usually sheer destruction is cheaper to achieve than preservation.

The answer to these equations depends on what the defence wants to achieve. President Reagan's maximum goal of a defence that would negate the ballistic missile — in other words, where it is cities that must be protected, a virtually "leak-proof" defence — sets the most difficult standard. No one believes it can be achieved in this century — unless by some arms control agreement that severely limits the offence — and many believe it impossible in principle. Not merely is the task of intercepting a present day missile force difficult; there are many relatively easy ways to make the offence more robust against the defence. Decoy technology is fertile and fairly cheap. Elements in the defence system may be very vulnerable: radars, C^3, satellites. Boost interception by laser and to a lesser extent by other means may be thwarted by higher acceleration, "fast-burn" missiles that achieve full speed and even RV separation while still shrouded in the atmosphere. Simplest of all, offensive weapons can be multiplied.

The benefit of eliminating the threat of the ballistic missile must also be measured, of course, against the knowledge that there are other ways of delivering nuclear weapons, notably aircraft and cruise missiles. To defend population adequately, even a workable ABM system would have to be supplemented by air defences. In this respect there is a significant difference between the Soviet Union, which has never abandoned an elaborate air defence and the US which has.

Advocates of ABM argue that even "intermediate" systems would be useful, chiefly for the purpose once set the old Safeguard system: namely defending offensive weapons and thereby deterring pre-emptive attack by greatly increasing the uncertainty of success. Weapons are much easier to defend than people, not merely because they are more easily sheltered but because even partial success can be enough. By deploying defence "preferentially" around certain secretly selected targets, the enemy can be compelled to attack all targets as heavily as if they were all defended. Among the subjects for selective defence are the components of C^3I.

As the SDI programme made progress, sharp controversy broke out as to what is permitted short of denouncing the ABM Treaty. What is unquestioned is that deployment of an ABM system of interceptors

Below: The Soviet Union is developing a number of ground-based lasers in a programme estimated by US sources to cost $1 billion a year. Such lasers could be used to blind or attack satellites, destroy warheads or developed into a variety of tactical applications. The Soviet Union has already fielded laser systems capable of blinding aircrew on some warships and may produce other weapons for battlefield anti-personnel and anti-aircraft use.

Bottom of page: Electro-Magnetic Rail Gun. Small projectiles fired at extremely high speeds could easily destroy opposing missiles and warheads. One problem with this type of weapon is devising a homing warhead that is small enough and strong enough to survive being fired at the very high velocity forces that this type of weapon would need.

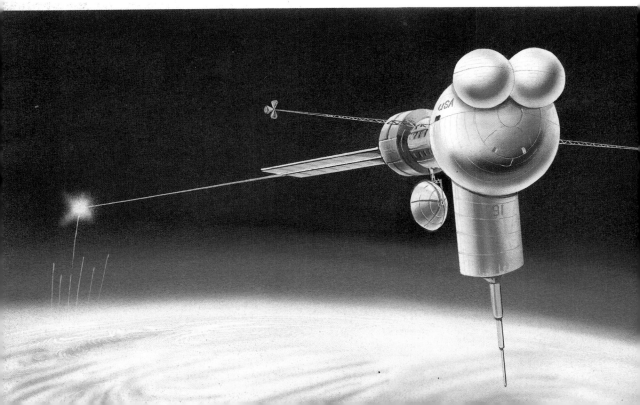

Page 49 Right

The use of ground-based lazers firing a beam up to space-based mirrors which then focuses it onto a rising ICBM is one idea actively being pursued by both Superpowers.

Below

Directed energy weapons in space would have a role against opposing satellites even if they were not deployed in sufficient numbers to provide a defence against ballistic missiles. The Soviet Union could have a prototype space-based anti-satelilite weapon by 1990 according to U.S. estimtates.

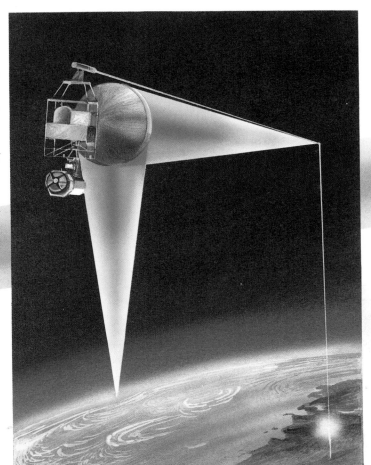

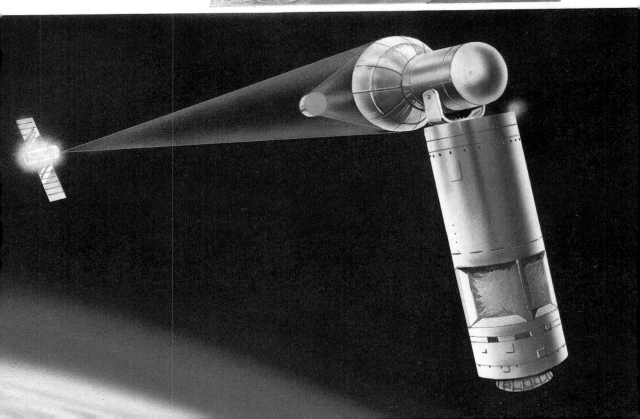

beyond a Russian system around Moscow or a US system in a missile field (the United States agreed with the Soviet Union that neither would deploy a second system as permitted by the Treaty) is banned. Research is permitted and so is testing of fixed components in designated testing areas. If systems not based on interceptor missiles (e.g. lasers) are "created", deployment must not be undertaken without discussion between the signatories. Another article prohibits development and testing of sea-based, air-based, space-based and mobile land-based "ABM systems and ABM components".

Proponents of a "broad interpretation" of the Treaty argue that this article bans development of all components of systems, even if based on new principles. Those who take a narrow interpretation argue that anything other than interceptor systems can be taken to the point of "creation", i.e. as full systems, before becoming liable to the requirement of discussion before deployment.

Which interpretation is chosen has a major implication for how far SDI and other programmes can go without breaching a treaty that many regard as a cornerstone of strategic stability. For opponents of strategic defence and believers in vulnerability as the paradoxical basis of stability, the issue is a crucial one. Even for many others a unilateral breach or denunciation of the ABM Treaty would seem a retrograde step. Nevertheless, as so often, the inexorable pressure of technology tends to change the shape of political relations.

The new radar at Pushkin controlling interceptions of incoming warheads is a large "phased array" — i.e. the familiar mechanically rotating, vulnerable and limited capacity antenna is replaced by pulses phased over a fixed, sloping electronic array. Newest feature of the active defence is the high acceleration Gazelle interceptor designed to wait until the atmosphere has made it easier to distinguish light decoys from real warheads.

Missile Defence of Moscow

The only fully operational anti-missile defence system in the world is deployed around Moscow. Somewhat run down after the earlier enthusiasm of the late 1960s, the system was upgraded to the permitted ceiling of 100 launchers in a programme beginning in 1978. The new system is designed to have two layers of interceptors in a pattern reminiscent of the abandoned US Safeguard. Exoatmospheric interception is provided by modernised Galosh missiles, now silo-based, while closer in, endoatmospheric cover is assigned to silo-based, high acceleration Gazelle missiles. It is possible that the silos can be reloaded after use.

A new radar serves for managing the defence. Warning, detection and tracking is provided by a combination of satellites to detect launch; Henhouse phased array radars now being replaced afford further ballistic missile warning. It is the building of one of these at Krasnoyarsk in Siberia, i.e. not on the periphery of the USSR as required by the ABM Treaty, that the US believes to be a breach of the agreement, designed to provide target tracking appropriate to an ABM system rather than mere warning. The only permitted radars for battle management must be within 150 kilometres of the capital. Because the phased array radars are the long-lead time component of ABM systems, the United States fears evasion of the restrictions would permit a rapid "breakout" by deployment of the more easily concealed anti-ballistic missiles.

The Soviet Union, unlike the United States, takes advantage of deployment of a missile defence for the national capital permitted by the 1972 ABM Treaty as amended. Facilities other than early warning radars for this are confined to within 150 km (93 miles) of the national capital. This system accords with the high value placed by the Soviet Union on the defence of the centres of political power. While the NATO nuclear powers could probably penetrate this defence, their task is complicated both technically — the UK has spent over a billion pounds on a re-entry vehicle intended to preserve a capability against Moscow — and strategically, e.g. uncertainty about the performance of the system would make it difficult to "size" limited attacks.

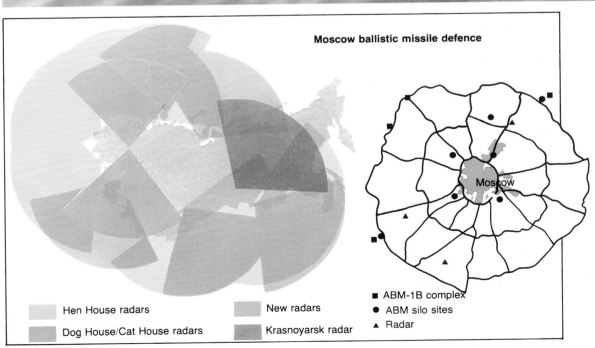

Moscow ballistic missile defence

Hen House radars

Dog House/Cat House radars

New radars

Krasnoyarsk radar

■ ABM-1B complex
● ABM silo sites
▲ Radar

Europe Under Threat

Modern Europe houses the most powerful concentration of armed forces the world has ever seen, including the largest collection of nuclear weapons dedicated to regional use. This is the consequence of the collapse of the European balance of power that for several centuries constituted the pivot of world politics. At the end of World War II the Soviet Union had mobilised an immense army and brought it forward into Central Europe. Uneasy jockeying for position in such early post-war crises as the Communist coup in Czechoslovakia and the Berlin Blockade established a provisional limit on the advance of Soviet power at the "Iron Curtain" that now divides the Warsaw Pact from NATO, but even after economic recovery, political division has prevented any indigenous centre of European power emerging capable of establishing a military balance with the Soviet Union. Moreover, so long as Soviet power contains a nuclear element, a particular problem arises from the status of the Federal Republic of Germany as the most powerful element within NATO but pledged for historic reasons not to possess nuclear weapons of its own; a pledge the abandonment of which would almost inevitably cause a major crisis.

The solution to this imbalance has been the introduction of American military power to Europe on a permanent basis within the North Atlantic Alliance. At first this introduction was chiefly characterised by the appoinment of an American Supreme Commander, Europe (SACEUR), and the reinforcement of residual US occupation troops into a peacetime garrison expeditionary force. But even in 1949, when the North Atlantic Treaty was signed, the United States was a nuclear power and although atomic weapons were too limited in numbers and power and too difficult to deliver to serve as a full scale nuclear guarantee of the kind we have since come to conceive, it was clear that if the Soviet Union went to war with the United States over Europe, it would suffer nuclear bombing.

None of this was very clearly thought through at the time or adequately debated in public. In subsequent years, however, the issues have given rise to recurrent controversy and the official doctrines of NATO have changed several times and continue to do so.

In the first revisionist phase, the heavy costs of undertaking the build-up of conventional forces thought necessary by NATO leaders, once the Korean War had given the impression that Soviet aggression might be more imminent than previously suspected, bred disillusionment with trying to counter the Red Army on its own terms. At the same time the advent of "nuclear plenty" made it seem that the United States had a big advantage both in strategic nuclear weapons and in smaller weapons that could be spared for tactical purposes. The United States therefore announced a strategy emphasising nuclear weapons as an "equaliser" for Soviet conventional strength. This strategy suggested — though it did not promise — that Soviet aggression would be met by nuclear attacks — "Massive Retaliation" — on the Soviet Union, a price the latter was not expected to pay. At the same time in 1954 SACEUR was given authority to plan on the assumption that if war came NATO would use nuclear weapons.

The United States nuclear guarantee to Europe creates complicated problems for systems of command, for while American weapons are theoretically available to serve European interests, the United States' President retains absolute authority over the use of such weapons and will clearly have US national interests in mind. Thus in the case of the Ground Launched Cruise Missiles (GLCMs) deployed in Europe during the 1980s, a network of electronic links permits commanders to seek the release of the weapons through both the NATO chain of command via SHAPE and the US HQ of European Command (EUCOM) which controls the central USAF base at Ramstein. NATO guidelines would require a parallel consultation between the President and the heads of government of the ally in which the particular GLCMs were based and on whose territory (if any) they were to be detonated.

This strategy soon ran into practical and political difficulties. Soviet acquisition of thermonuclear weapons and the prospect if not yet the reality of effective delivery systems — a prospect made much more vivid by the launch of Sputnik in 1957 — suggested that if the United States used nuclear weapons on the Soviet Union, it would receive them in return. At the same time, well-publicised exercises revealed that if NATO handled this problem in part by using nuclear weapons to halt the Red Army on the battlefield, Europeans would suffer huge casualties even without taking account of possible Soviet nuclear retaliation in kind.

Massive Retaliation and the idea of nuclear war fighting in Europe consequently underwent a crisis of credibility. Nuclear disarmament movements arose and the strategy came to appear a transparent bluff that would lead in a crisis, according to the 1960 Democratic presidential candidate J. F. Kennedy, to either "Holocaust or Humiliation".

By this time one reaction had been the appearance of a British national nuclear force and a French decision to acquire one. This was to provide the basis for policies of trying to establish national nuclear sanctuaries by individual policies of massive retaliation. The United States itself began to move towards a more cautious policy in which the nuclear response to aggression would be delayed while less drastic ways of repelling aggression were tried; this trend was to result in the withdrawal of France from the military organisation of NATO, for fear of

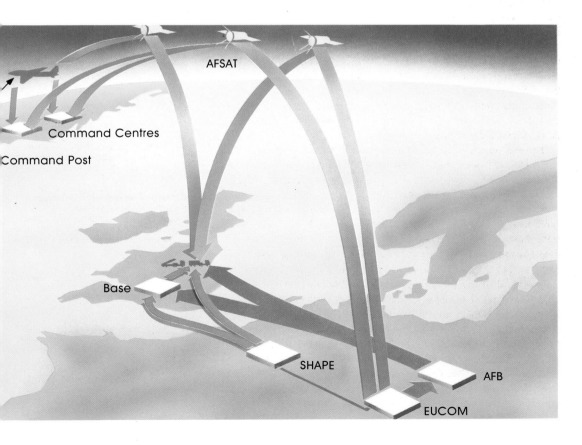

Command Centres

Command Post

AFSAT

Base

SHAPE

EUCOM

AFB

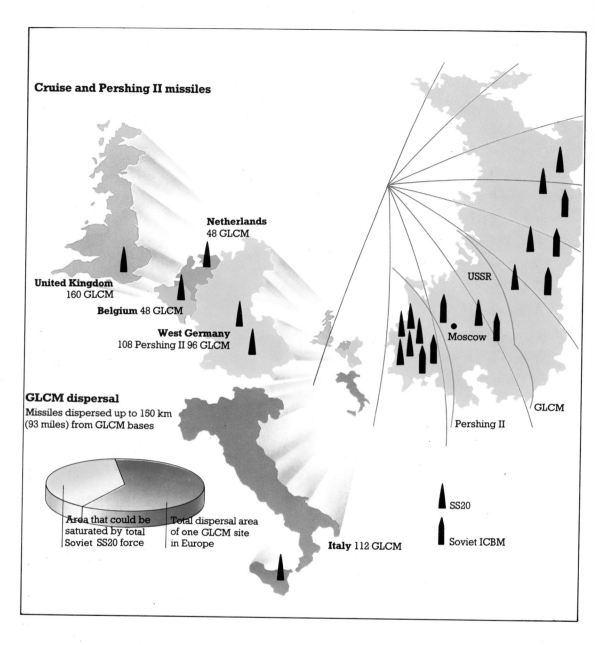

Cruise and Pershing II missiles

Netherlands
48 GLCM

United Kingdom
160 GLCM

Belgium 48 GLCM

West Germany
108 Pershing II 96 GLCM

USSR

Moscow

GLCM

Pershing II

GLCM dispersal
Missiles dispersed up to 150 km
(93 miles) from GLCM bases

SS20

Soviet ICBM

Area that could be
saturated by total
Soviet SS20 force

Total dispersal area
of one GLCM site
in Europe

Italy 112 GLCM

being embroiled in a nuclear war confined to Europe while the Superpowers went unscathed, and the subsequent adoption by NATO, in 1967, of the strategy of "flexible response", still its official doctrine.

Before that, in an abortive effort to reassure Europeans that their interests would be taken into account and safeguarded, the United States tried to set up a Multilateral Nuclear Force, ultimately in the proposed form of a force of submarines, armed with nuclear weapons of the Polaris type and manned by multinational crews. The weapons would still be subject, however, to US control under a two-key system. Such a system had already been used when the United States deployed

The diagram shows the deployment concept of the US GLCM in Europe. Deployment in several countries affords both a degree of security and a political symbolism of solidarity. Upon dispersal from bases, the very mobile missiles could quickly create a very difficult targeting problem for the Soviet Union unless locations could be reliably tracked by satellite or agents. The problem would not merely be the number of warheads required for a saturation area attack but the escalatory consequences of doing so.

intermediate range ballistic missiles to Britain (Thor) and Italy and Turkey (Jupiter).

This idea failed to win support both because of the cost and, more important, the European belief that it did not significantly add to their strategic leverage. While it might not have done so physically, management of the force would inevitably have compelled the United States to share more nuclear knowledge with its allies. After de Gaulle's departure, this purpose was served with considerable effectiveness by setting up, in 1966, a Nuclear Planning Group (NPG), which has proved a valuable forum for consultation. A few Polaris SSBN were also assigned for use by SACEUR.

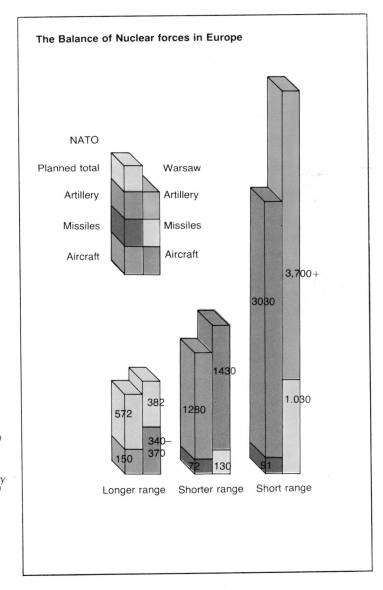

The Balance of Nuclear forces in Europe

NATO

Planned total — Warsaw

Artillery — Artillery

Missiles — Missiles

Aircraft — Aircraft

572   382
150   340—
       370

1280   1430
72   130

3030   3,700+
        1,030
91

Longer range   Shorter range   Short range

Theatre nuclear weapons have become both an important factor in the European military balance and a major focus for arms control negotiation. The Soviet Union constructed itself superiority in all categories with a heavy preponderance in the mid-range of 500-1000 miles (800-1600 km) and a markedly greater preference for ballistic missiles.

Nevertheless, NATO's nuclear strategy remains under strain. In the first place, the Soviet capacity to devastate the United States and thus exact a terrible price if the Americans used nuclear weapons on Europe's behalf is now established beyond question. Secondly, the Soviet Union has maintained a fair margin of conventional superiority over NATO, so that the latter still cannot renounce the use of nuclear weapons to compensate. Thirdly, the Soviet Union has transformed the situation in recent years by greatly strengthening its once rather neglected tactical and theatre nuclear forces.

In the early days of its missile programme the Soviet Union built up a large force of intermediate range missiles (IRBM) capable of devastating Western Europe, China and Japan. Ever since those days, Western Europe has been under a nuclear threat, including, of course, one from aircraft, although IRBMs came to occupy a relatively less important role in Soviet strategy as its ICBM and SLBM forces improved. In the 1970s, however, the Soviet Union began to replace its ageing and vulnerable IRBMs with a new, mobile, MIRVd IRBM, the SS20, and to re-equip its armed forces with a new family of short and medium range missiles (SS21, SS22 and SS23).

This effort served both to remind the Western Europeans of their vulnerability in war and to make it clear that it was by no means certain that it would pay NATO even militarily to resort to using nuclear weapons. A basic element in the flexible response was thus thrown into question. Moreover by refurbishing its capability to devastate Western Europe with forces quite distinct from those aimed at the United States, the Soviet Union somewhat revived the old European fear of getting involved in a nuclear war that spared American and Russian territory.

The Soviet Union, once geographically relatively impregnable, is open to attack from all sides in the air and missile age. Moreover it faces several nuclear powers that it regards as hostile. In response, it has constructed itself a formidable array of missile, air, land and sea forces, manning all its frontiers and providing a powerful, long range striking force. Despite long coastlines, climatic and geographical conditions make egress for Soviet naval forces extremely difficult.

USA SLBMs

USA SLBMs

Pac
Tot
Nav

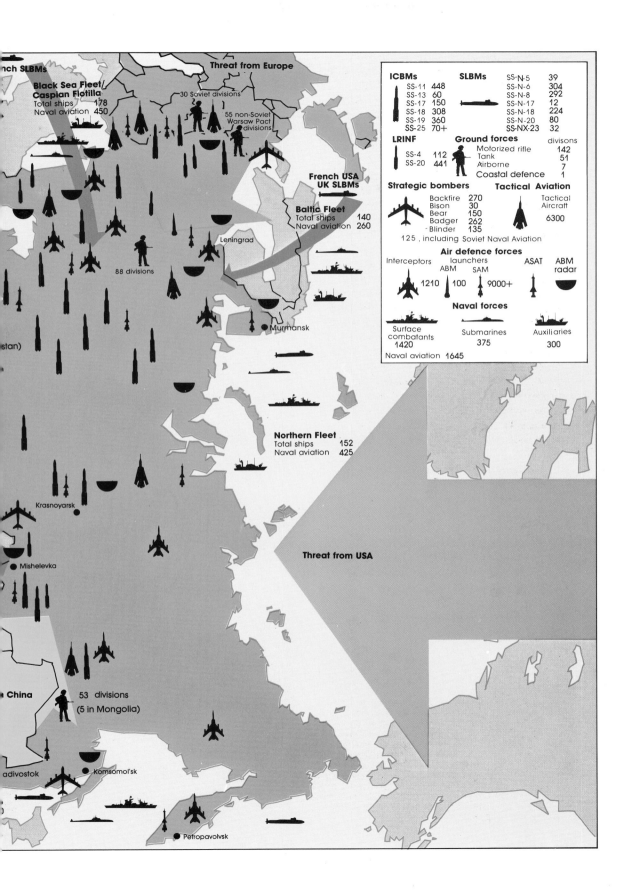

ICBMs
SS-11 448
SS-13 60
SS-17 150
SS-18 308
SS-19 360
SS-25 70+

SLBMs
SS-N-5 39
SS-N-6 304
SS-N-8 292
SS-N-17 12
SS-N-18 224
SS-N-20 80
SS-NX-23 32

LRINF
SS-4 112
SS-20 441

Ground forces divisons
Motorized rifle 142
Tank 51
Airborne 7
Coastal defence 1

Strategic bombers
Backfire 270
Bison 30
Bear 150
Badger 262
Blinder 135
125 , including Soviet Naval Aviation

Tactical Aviation
Tactical Aircraft 6300

Air defence forces
Interceptors 1210
launchers ABM 100
SAM 9000+
ASAT
ABM radar

Naval forces
Surface combatants 1420
Submarines 375
Auxiliaries 300
Naval aviation 1645

nch SLBMs

Black Sea Fleet/ Caspian Flotilla
Total ships 178
Naval aviation 450

Threat from Europe

30 Soviet divisions

55 non-Soviet Warsaw Pact divisions

French USA UK SLBMs

Baltic Fleet
Total ships 140
Naval aviation 260

Leningrad

88 divisions

Murmansk

stan)

Northern Fleet
Total ships 152
Naval aviation 425

Krasnoyarsk

Mishelevka

Threat from USA

China
53 divisions
(5 in Mongolia)

adivostok

Komsomol'sk

Petropavolvsk

It was in part to solve this political problem that NATO responded in 1979 to the SS20 deployment by agreeing to the stationing in Europe of American Ground Launched Cruise Missiles and Pershing II.

Like the Soviet Union, NATO has long possessed some shorter range nuclear missiles, with US warheads under two-key control, nuclear aircraft and nuclear artillery. Europe thus has the potential to become a major nuclear battleground. By the 1980s, however, the weight of strategic opinion at NATO was coming to accept that no widespread or heavy use of these weapons is compatible with European interests. Because nuclear weapons are surprisingly ineffective against military forces on the battlefield unless used in large numbers — whereupon the battle would probably lose all coherence — the trend is to think in terms of the selective use of small numbers of weapons, probably of longer range, in the attempt to have a favourable effect on the war, but more fundamentally to persuade the aggressor it would be too dangerous to continue.

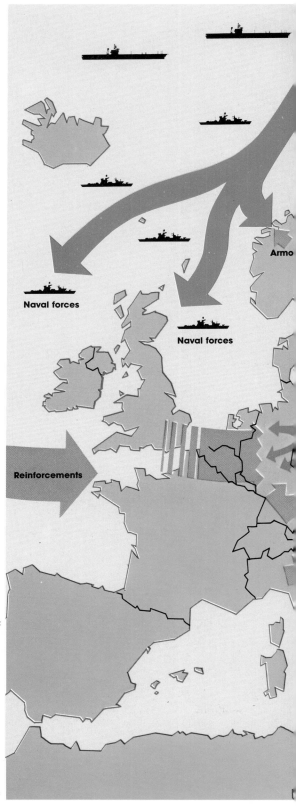

The overall pattern of a general war in Europe would probably take the form of a major Warsaw Pact invasion westward across the North German Plain, conducted by successive waves of ground forces and met by an initial "covering" NATO resistance hopefully rapidly stiffened by reinforcements from across the Atlantic. Soviet forces might attempt flanking operations in Scandinavia and the Mediterranean, supported by naval forces that would try to break out and also impede NATO reinforcements. NATO naval forces, particularly the US strike fleets organised around carriers, would try to counter these operations and provide support for the land battle.

Armour

Amphibious
assault

Second
strategic
echelon

Armour

Armour

Armour

Armour

Naval forces

Naval forces

US 6th Fleet
under attack

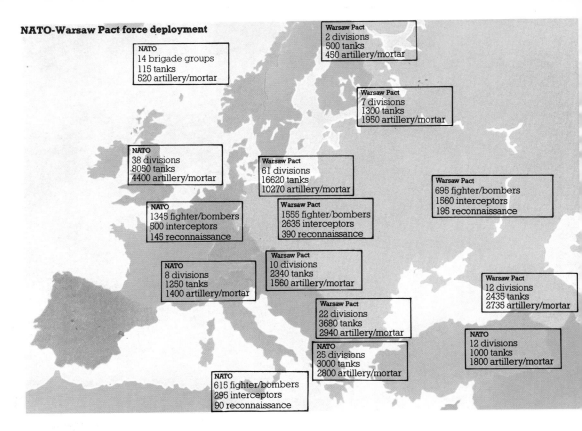

NATO
14 brigade groups
115 tanks
520 artillery/mortar

Warsaw Pact
2 divisions
500 tanks
450 artillery/mortar

Warsaw Pact
7 divisions
1300 tanks
1950 artillery/mortar

NATO
38 divisions
8050 tanks
4400 artillery/mortar

Warsaw Pact
61 divisions
16620 tanks
10270 artillery/mortar

Warsaw Pact
695 fighter/bombers
1560 interceptors
195 reconnaissance

NATO
1345 fighter/bombers
500 interceptors
145 reconnaissance

Warsaw Pact
1555 fighter/bombers
2635 interceptors
390 reconnaissance

NATO
8 divisions
1250 tanks
1400 artillery/mortar

Warsaw Pact
10 divisions
2340 tanks
1560 artillery/mortar

Warsaw Pact
12 divisions
2435 tanks
2735 artillery/mortar

Warsaw Pact
22 divisions
3680 tanks
2940 artillery/mortar

NATO
12 divisions
1000 tanks
1800 artillery/mortar

NATO
25 divisions
3000 tanks
2800 artillery/mortar

NATO
615 fighter/bombers
295 interceptors
90 reconnaissance

Nuclear Weapons in Europe's Strategy

Nuclear weapons have constituted the core of NATO's strategy for most of its existence. When the first Soviet nuclear test in August 1949 made it clear that the Soviet Union would be a nuclear power earlier than expected, the initial NATO reaction was to increase conventional forces to offset their Soviet equivalents by the time Soviet nuclear weapons were capable of neutralising American (and any other NATO member's) own nuclear weapons. The policy of major conventional rearmament was, however, expensive and unpopular. Consequently the Alliance soon reverted to reliance on nuclear weapons to deter all aggression. Indeed for a time the persisting American superiority in nuclear forces encouraged even greater reliance on nuclear weapons than before, so that the United States entered the period of Massive Retaliation and NATO commanders planned on using nuclear weapons from the start both on the battlefield and in a General Strike Plan (GSP) under the Supreme Commander Europe (SACEUR), a local version of the American strategic strike devised to attack targets especially significant for the European battle.

When the rise of Soviet nuclear power and popular fears about the consequences of nuclear war in Europe cast great doubt on the credibility or prudence of such reliance on nuclear weapons, the United States led its allies to adopt a new strategy of flexible response which still remains NATO strategy today. France refused to accept such notions and left the integrated military command structure to pursue a national version of massive retaliation on its own account.

Nevertheless NATO's flexible response is still at bottom a nuclear strategy. It calls for aggression to be met initially on its own terms, i.e. if it is conventional then efforts will be made to conduct a direct defence. If that begins to fail to the point at which the integrity of an ally or of the overall defence is endangered, then the strategy anticipates "deliberate escalation" by use of nuclear weapons. It is hoped that this will both bolster the defence and send a warning signal to re-establish deterrence. Should that fail, heavier nuclear action would theoretically occur up to the level of strategic war.

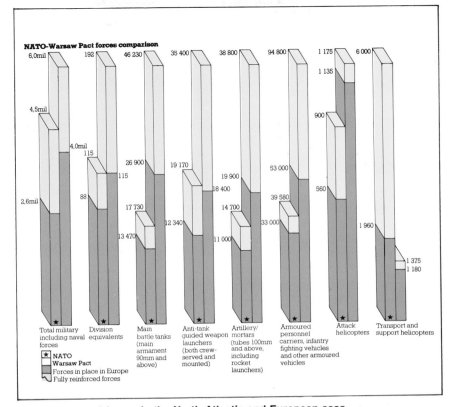

NATO – Warsaw Pact naval forces in the North Atlantic and European seas

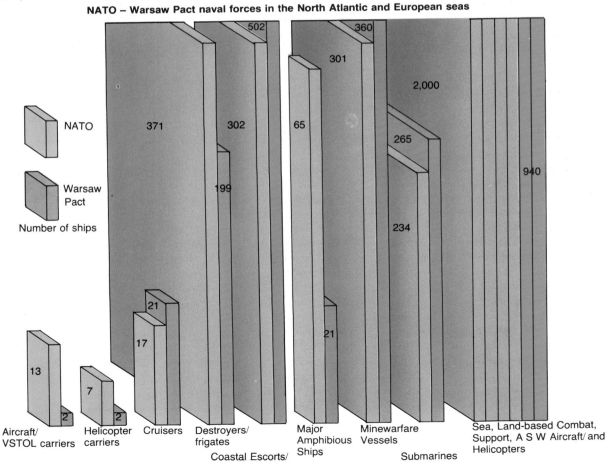

European Arsenals

Nuclear weapons enter strategic calculations for Europe in many different dimensions. Given the North Atlantic Treaty and the presence of hundreds of thousands of American troops in Europe within a NATO commanded by an American general, the umbrella guarantee extended by American strategic forces can never be wholly discounted by the Soviet Union. There are also the British and French national nuclear forces to consider. Thirdly come the nuclear weapons, chiefly American but also a few British and French, specifically dedicated to use in a European war. Many of the American warheads are in the hands of allied units under two-key control. Against these are arrayed the numerous comparable Soviet systems.

The official NATO strategy since 1967, laid down in Military Committee paper MC14/3, is "flexible response". Under this NATO would try to meet aggression confined to conventional weapons in kind, resorting to nuclear weapons only if the conventional resistance crumbled to the point at which the integrity of NATO forces or of the territory of a member of the alliance was in dire danger. However, the opinion of successive SACEURs has been that this moment could probably not be deferred more than a few days.

NATO's nuclear response is therefore a key part of its strategy. Unfortunately it is also very imperfect. When the alliance first fell back on the idea of using nuclear weapons to compensate for conventional inferiority, the United States enjoyed a virtual monopoly of such weapons and overwhelming superiority in strategic weapons to

The diagram schematises the flexible response and shows the overlapping roles in the implementation of the escalatory stages. Clearly the crucial phase is the controlled escalation in which conventional and nuclear forces work together. The colours of the arrows also tentatively suggest where the balance of advantage currently lies in the successive levels of force. This must be interpreted cautiously because the nuclear levels of force on either side are quite adequate to do devastating damage; the politico-strategic question is at what level an aggressor might desist, or a defender give up.

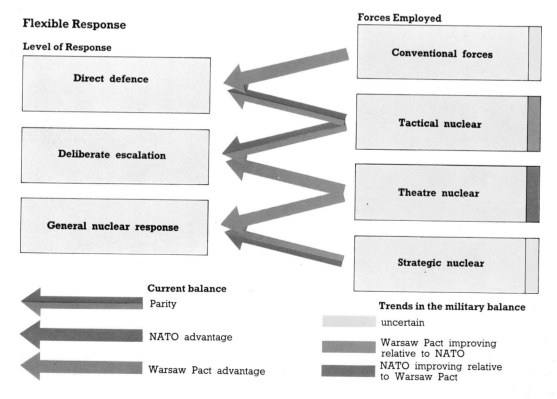

Flexible Response

Level of Response

- Direct defence
- Deliberate escalation
- General nuclear response

Forces Employed

- Conventional forces
- Tactical nuclear
- Theatre nuclear
- Strategic nuclear

Current balance

Parity

NATO advantage

Warsaw Pact advantage

Trends in the military balance

uncertain

Warsaw Pact improving relative to NATO

NATO improving relative to Warsaw Pact

discourage Soviet "escalation". Today the Soviet Union has decisively closed the gap. Also in the early days, the military were under no obligation to consider "collateral" damage in their plans, so that the consequences would have been quite unacceptable to friendly governments. Now that this omission has been rectified, it proves very difficult to develop effective ways to use nuclear weapons on the battlefield, though various technological remedies such as accuracy, smaller warheads and more "tailored" weapon effects are used in attempts to solve the problem. Meanwhile, many commanders doubt whether they would ever get permission to use nuclear weapons and tend not to count on them. For all these reasons there is something of a gap between NATO's official nuclear doctrine and what politicians and generals really expect. In partial response to this, NATO has set out on a modernisation programme designed to produce fewer weapons more in keeping with reality. The introduction of new weapons is, however, proving a very controversial political issue. Withdrawal of weapons is easier, and since the 1979 decision to deploy GLCM and Pershing II nearly 2000 short range nuclear weapons have been unilaterally withdrawn from NATO, particularly air defence weapons and nuclear land mines.

The diagram suggests the sequences by which an initial conventional aggression might proceed through escalatory stages to general nuclear war. Flexible response hopes to use these stages in a controlled way to terminate aggression before the final catastrophe, but the stages could, of course, follow each other in an uncontrolled way to the bitter end. The diagrams also remind us that it may not be left to NATO to take the nuclear initiative. Indeed, it can be argued that if the Soviet Union takes flexible response seriously and still decides to attack, its best course might be to go nuclear from the start to disarm NATO.

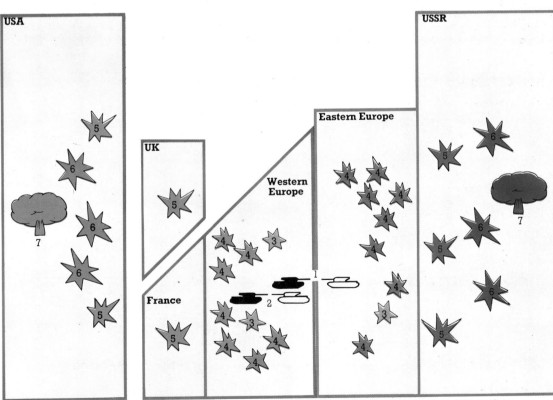

1. Conventional forces clash.
2. NATO falls back. Holds? Unable to force Soviets to retreat? Or faces imminent defeat.
3. NATO escalates to nuclear weapons – demonstrative strike to show risks Soviets run? *Or* Soviets decide to go nuclear to breakthrough.
4. Tactical nuclear weapons used in large numbers.
5. Selective nuclear strikes extend to USSR, rear areas and USA.
6. Limited nuclear war breaks out between the superpowers.
7. General nuclear war.

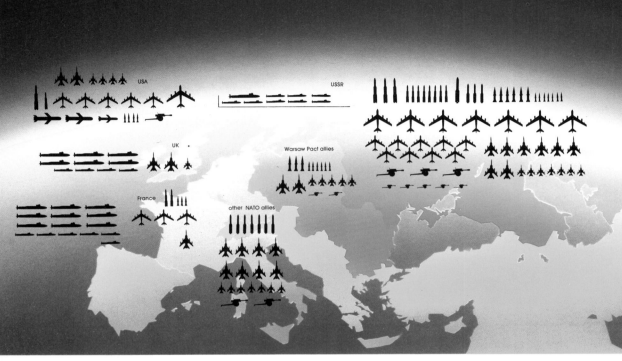

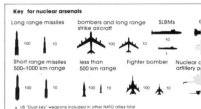

Nuclear Coupling

Europe houses a vast array of nuclear forces, the use of even a half of which would do catastrophic damage to all concerned. The forces are, of course, intended to strike a balance so that this never occurs. Without nuclear weapons, at least unless and until there is very much greater progress toward political unification and military integration, Western Europe is hopelessly out-gunned by the Soviet Union. For several decades, therefore, NATO has existed to bring the United States into the balance.

The current form of NATO strategy rests upon a policy of escalation if necessary to the use of strategic nuclear weapons. While Britain and France have such weapons they are on a small scale compared to the Soviet Union and not well suited to execute or cover a first strike. Consequently the key question for NATO is whether American strategic weapons are reliably "coupled" to European defence — coupled sufficiently credibly to deter Soviet attack.

The structure of nuclear forces itself is a major, perhaps the chief mechanism to secure this coupling. But it is not the only link. For the nuclear forces are bound up in a complex political and military relationship; indeed if they were not, the nuclear structure itself would probably lack credibility and even collapse.

We should not underestimate the binding effect of the North Atlantic Treaty itself. Although merely a piece of paper and lacking even a firm pledge that the allies will go to war for each other, it is widely regarded as the world's most solemn and important alliance. Not to honour it would deal American prestige and power a devastating blow. Thus, if aggression took place, the Treaty would probably get the United States into the war.

Another link is, of course, the garrison of hundreds of thousands of American forces under arms in Europe, which would have to be overrun by an attack. The current posture of flexible response requires those forces to possess many nuclear weapons; these too would have to be attacked or overrun. Moreover these weapons are there to execute nuclear strikes if conventional resistance fails. The use of even a few would cross an ominous dividing line beyond which escalation would be in one sense quantitative and no longer qualitative.

Of course the ominousness of this line would make the United States reluctant to cross it for fear of retaliation. It is fear that this inhibition would prevail that raises the fear that American nuclear power has been or is becoming decoupled from European defence. The Soviet Union has worked to achieve such decoupling by building up its strategic power to deter American attacks on the Soviet Union, building up theatre nuclear forces so as to deny NATO military advantage in going nuclear at that level, and by redesigning its conventional forces for much more rapid offensive action, thus opening up the possibility of winning before the United States can even decide to go nuclear.

It was to counter these moves that the United States agreed with its allies that it would modernise its theatre nuclear forces and in particular introduce missiles in the Intermediate Nuclear Force range so as to:

(1)   match equivalent Soviet forces which otherwise threatened Europe in a way that could not otherwise be matched without using strategic forces or vulnerable aircraft;

(2)   make it possible to involve Soviet territory in a theatre war;

(3)   base the capability to do this symbolically on the territory it was to defend;

(4)   do so in clear-cut American ownership and operation;

(5)   have the potential to raise theatre war to a level that already would have implications for the later strategic phases, e.g. targets relevant to strategic nuclear war might be engaged;

(6)   symbolise the continuum from local tactical nuclear action to strategic nuclear war.

The INF were thus a central link in the escalatory chain, designed to couple US nuclear power to Europe. But that link would not be credible if not set in the context of all the other means for ensuring that a Soviet attack could not prevail without a serious war and that the United States could scarcely escape being drawn into that war. In practice, such are the risks, that various links in this mesh of coupling could become rusty without greatly weakening deterrence. But visible effort to keep the links in good order is a major demonstration of common will and thus in itself a reinforcement of the coupling mechanism.

Nuclear Release

The problem of how to release nuclear weapons for actual use is both difficult and important. From the very beginning of the nuclear age the new weapons were recognised to be of a different order; for many years the American armed forces did not have custody of warheads in peace time, a taboo broken down by the advent of the missile requiring permanent mating of warhead to vehicle. All governments take special precautions to ensure that nuclear weapons can only be used with the highest political authority. On the other hand, a weapon cannot be effective in war unless it is available at the right place and time, or serve as a deterrent unless it is known that it would be so.

Electronic controls and codes have made it somewhat easier to disperse weapons while retaining a physical veto over their use. There remains, however, the difficult strategic and political problem of deciding when to release the weapons for use and of ensuring that the capability reaches the user's hands in time. This problem is complicated in NATO by the need for two or more governments to agree. The so-called "Athens guidelines" agreed by NATO in 1962, and since updated, require consultation before use if "time and circumstances" permit.

The original concept of release in NATO was "bottom up"; that is, a commander believing he needs to use nuclear weapons and believing that he would be justified, sends a request up through the military chain of command. In NATO this is twofold, one American (except where the few British weapons are concerned; French weapons are not dedicated to NATO), the other an alliance chain to SACEUR. SACEUR, being both NATO's Supreme Commander and the American C-in-C, would consult both NATO's political leadership and the US President. If authority were granted it would be passed back to the would-be user with the necessary codes to release the weapon.

This procedure would be time-consuming, especially under wartime conditions. Moreover there is a real danger that the signal traffic involved might be detected and assessed by the enemy as a signal that nuclear use was imminent and thereby allow him to pre-empt. In recent years there has therefore been a growing school of thought which believes that release should be "top-down"; in other words that the decision to "go nuclear" will in any case be a major political decision based not on the local state of the battle but on the general plight of the alliance. Consequently release is more likely to be taken at the highest levels with execution delegated to some subordinate commander. Many of the worst problems of release at least as a technical challenge would thereby be greatly eased.

The diagram shows the chain of alliance and national command for nuclear weapons in NATO. In the classic model, requests flow up from Corps level to SACEUR and on to political authority. Release and use authority follow down both alliance and national (chiefly US) chains. In top-down release consultation at the highest levels alone might initiate release and orders to use nuclear weapons. A parallel national process exists for French forces. In extremis the alliance as such cannot rule out unilateral use by the United States or another nuclear ally. As the crisis of the battle is most likely to arise in Germany or on the Flanks, the current climate in NATO suggests that extreme reluctance to act is likely to characterise all political parties to the process. The present procedure for nuclear release is so complex that it might be unworkable under war conditions; the full interallied consultation could scarcely take less than 24 hours. As the diagram shows, the US national chain of command could cut through all this if desired. In practice the United States might be reluctant rather than over-eager to go nuclear to save Europe.

Nuclear release

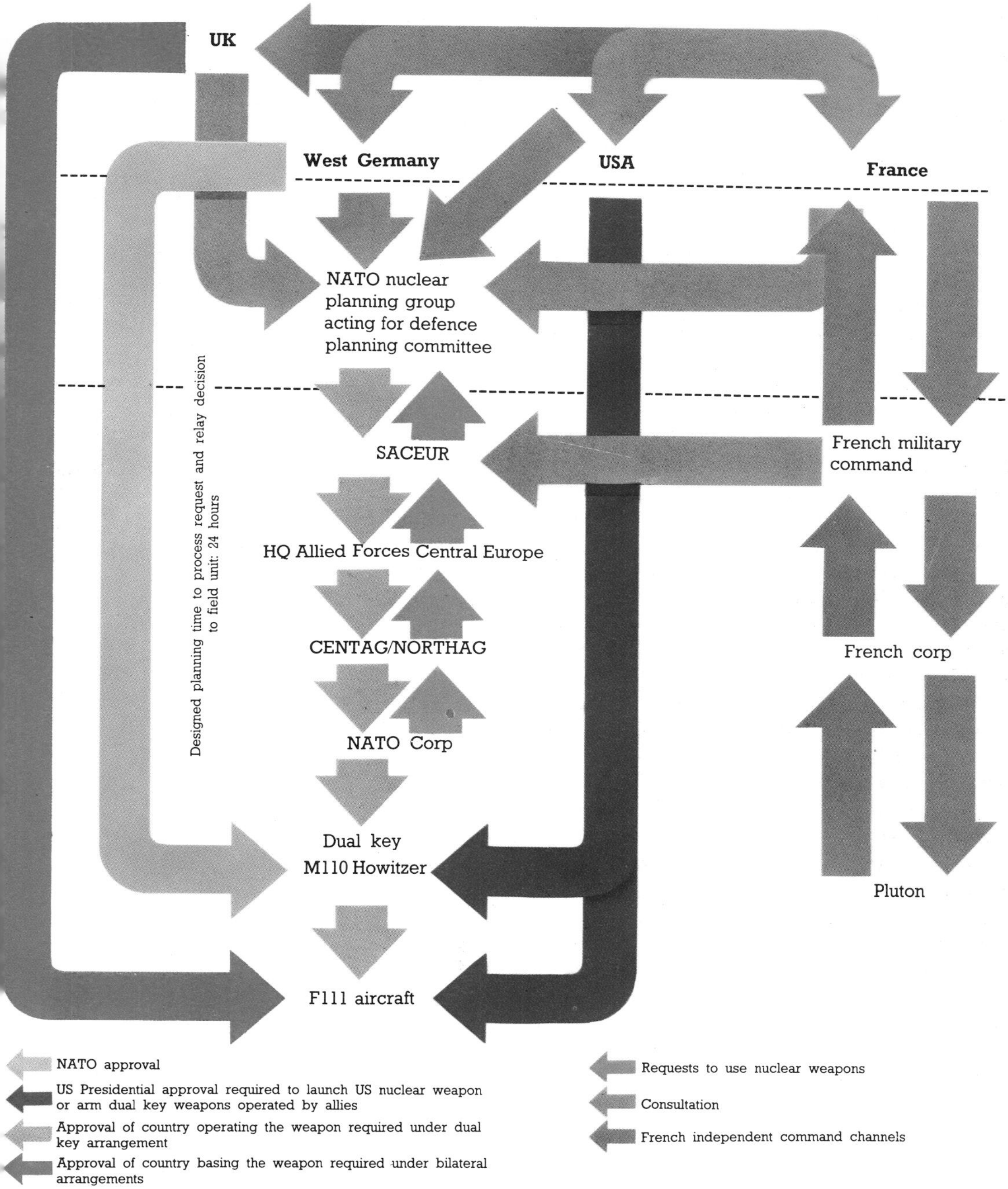

UK

West Germany

USA

France

NATO nuclear
planning group
acting for defence
planning committee

SACEUR

French military
command

HQ Allied Forces Central Europe

CENTAG/NORTHAG

French corp

NATO Corp

Dual key
M110 Howitzer

Pluton

F111 aircraft

Designed planning time to process request and relay decision
to field unit: 24 hours

NATO approval

US Presidential approval required to launch US nuclear weapon
or arm dual key weapons operated by allies

Approval of country operating the weapon required under dual
key arrangement

Approval of country basing the weapon required under bilateral
arrangements

Requests to use nuclear weapons

Consultation

French independent command channels

Franco-British Forces

The British and French national nuclear forces now serve somewhat similar strategic roles and are increasingly spoken of as the possible nucleus of a "European" nuclear force. The two forces have, however, very different conceptual origins and the residue of these still presents severe obstacles to collaboration.

British scientists played a major part in stimulating and then realising the American World War II project to develop a nuclear weapon. After the war, however, the United States rapidly cut off collaboration. The British Labour Government — or, rather, a small group within it — took it for granted that Britain must obtain this powerful new weapon and launched a national development programme. It was, however, always a major purpose of this programme to convince the United States of the advantages of renewing co-operation on nuclear questions, and Britain pursued a consistent, bipartisan policy of loyal collaboration within NATO.

French scientists also played a part, albeit much smaller, in the American Manhattan Project, but French nationalism, exacerbated by memory of defeat, lack of immediate resources, and the strong role of the Communist Party in France, all combined to defer a serious military nuclear programme and to inhibit both sides from the possibility of close collaboration with the United States. Indeed, it was in a mood of anti-Americanism following the Suez crisis that the French Government, under the socialist Premier Mendes-France, took the final decision in 1958 to proceed to build a national nuclear force. This decision, inherited almost immediately by de Gaulle, became the basis for an assertively nationalist nuclear strategy theory for the *force de frappe*, later *force de dissuasion*, and for French withdrawal in 1966 from the integrated military command of NATO.

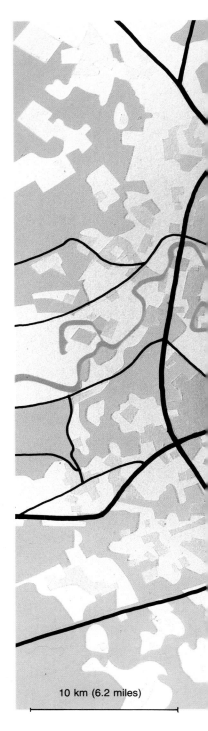

The question of whether a small nuclear force can constitute an effective deterrent depends for an answer on many variables including whom it is designed to deter and over what issues. In any particular case it may not be prudent to execute what was once thought to be the classic retaliatory strike on cities, for that might bring catastrophic and by definition heavier retaliation. Even a small nuclear force may therefore wish to begin with some form of limited, perhaps counter-military strike; in which case it must take steps to preserve the adequacy of its residual force of last resort. Nevertheless the map shows that it would not take many delivered warheads to constitute a devastating final blow. The circles show the area of Moscow that would receive five psi blast over-pressure from an optimal airburst weapon of typical French or British size: the orange circles depict the damage radii for one 150 kt warhead of the French M4 SLBM and the single 1 MT warhead of the IRBM S3 respectively: the red circle represents the 40 kt warhead of a

10 km (6.2 miles)

British Chevaline Polaris. Even if the smallest of these circles does not suggest a decisive blow, it would be a major disaster. If two or three arriving warheads might be tolerable, a couple of dozen fairly clearly would not be.

3.7 km (2.3 mile) radius

2.4 km (1.5 mile) radius

7.1 km (4.4 mile) radius

As a result of this history, the strategy and the rhetoric of the British and French national nuclear forces are very different and their significance within the Western alliance correspondingly distinctive. British governments have always depicted the British force as a "contribution to the Western deterrent". Explanations of how this contribution works have varied over time. Having succeeded in winning the renewed American technological collaboration they have always sought, the British co-ordinate targeting with the US SAC. When the American force was smaller it was possible to present the British V-bomber force as a useful quantitative addition to the joint capability; it was also said that there were targets of special interest to the United Kingdom, e.g. nuclear weapons believed to be aimed at Britain or submarine bases endangering British supply routes. In more recent years much weight has been laid on creating "multiple centres of decision" so that the Soviet Union will be uncertain of how far it dare push an aggression: a consideration very important within the NATO strategy of flexible response. This enables the United Kingdom to credit its national force with a role in offsetting any unreliability in the American nuclear guarantee without actively questioning American good faith. Thus the argument goes that the *British* have no doubts about American reliability but the *Russians* might underestimate it; in that case the existence of an independent British capacity to go nuclear will give them pause.

The British and French nuclear forces are far from negligible even though the limited numbers of submarines that carry the most powerful and invulnerable missiles renders them more susceptible to Soviet ASW than the large American forces. The existence of the latter does, of course, prevent the Soviet Union devoting a large portion of its effort to dealing with the lesser powers. Both France and Britain are engaged in major modernisation programmes that will greatly increase the number of available warheads. Independent British tactical nuclear forces are not numerous but the French arsenal is quite sizeable even if the penetration capability of the airborne portion may be debatable.

The French theory is very different. According to so-called "gaullist" thinking, the special deterrent value of nuclear weapons is to threaten catastrophic consequences to an aggressor. In a bipolar nuclear confrontation these consequences would be mutual. This serves the possible victim of aggression well, for the aggressor will never wish to pay the price and thus the defender will never have to do so either. Moreover since the aggressor will weigh the consequences of attack against the benefits of "winning", a lesser power needs only a lesser nuclear force. It must, however, be his own force, because the use of it would be suicidal and no nation will commit suicide for another. Thus the force must be quite independent in operation and, so far as possible, in construction.

Over the years, the evolution of the British and French nuclear forces has played a major part in alliance diplomacy. The United States initially tried to dissuade its allies from maintaining independent nuclear forces. The primary reason was, of course, a preference for keeping control of such dangerous instruments; a subsidiary but important reason was the anomalous position in which the Federal Republic of Germany found itself as increasingly the most powerful military partner for the United States, but denuclearised by treaty and by historical memory. On the other hand the United States had to do business with its nuclear allies. The paradox probably reached its extreme in 1962 when, in one year, the Secretary of Defense, Robert McNamara issued a famous warning against the dangers and uselessness of minor nuclear forces, first secretly in a NATO meeting at Athens and later publicly in a speech, while President Kennedy at Nassau acknowledged the success of British efforts to regain collaborative status by agreeing to sell Polaris missiles to the United Kingdom. By 1974, the United States was going along with NATO resolutions acknowledging the valuable contribution of the British and French forces to European security.

Arms control restrictions on American theatre weapons render the Franco-British forces more significant in NATO strategy, while deep cuts in Soviet and American strategic forces would also make it increasingly difficult to leave the "lesser" forces out of the equations.

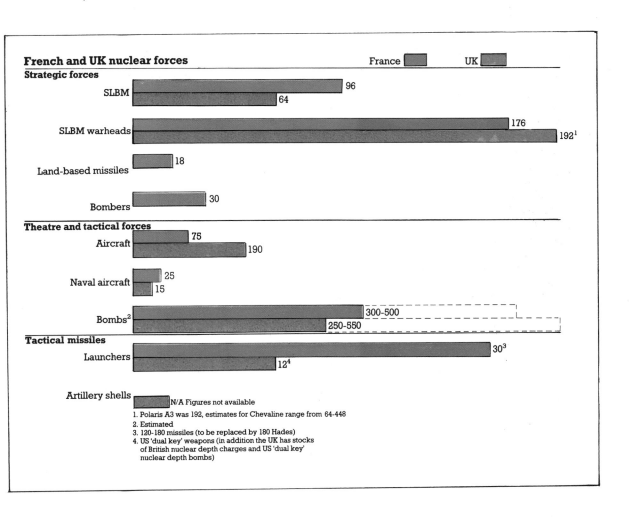

French and UK nuclear forces   France   UK

Strategic forces

SLBM — 96 / 64

SLBM warheads — 176 / 192[1]

Land-based missiles — 18

Bombers — 30

Theatre and tactical forces

Aircraft — 75 / 190

Naval aircraft — 25 / 15

Bombs[2] — 300-500 / 250-550

Tactical missiles

Launchers — 30[3] / 12[4]

Artillery shells — N/A Figures not available

1. Polaris A3 was 192, estimates for Chevaline range from 64-448
2. Estimated
3. 120-180 missiles (to be replaced by 180 Hades)
4. US 'dual key' weapons (in addition the UK has stocks of British nuclear depth charges and US 'dual key' nuclear depth bombs)

The national forces do, however, face serious problems. In gross power they have become considerable, and current modernisation programmes will make them more so. Since the retirement of its long-serving V-bomber force the United Kingdom has relied on Polaris A3 missiles purchased from the United States and based in submarines of US design. The re-entry vehicles and warheads — now a three MRV named Chevaline — are of British design and manufacture. Replacement by Trident II (D5) will continue this tradition; British spokesmen always maintain this dependence does not erode the operational independence of the force. Britain possesses some freefall bombs for tactical use but relies chiefly on American weapons for this level of combat; indeed, more broadly speaking, the British force is one of last resort, with reliance being placed on the collaborative NATO flexible response for the earlier stages of deterrence and defence.

French forces are almost entirely of French design and manufacture, though some American technology has come into French possession. When the force was very limited, France officially scorned the idea of a tactical phase of nuclear war, but as the French have entered their own age of comparative plenty they have developed tactical weapons. Their force thus comprises a mini-Triad of SLBMs, now modernising with the M4 MIRVd missiles, IRBMs, an airborne delivery capability, and two tactical missiles, the Pluton and the newly developed Hades. As this variegated capability has become available, and as for diplomatic reasons France has thought it prudent to be more openly a contributor to the defence of West Germany as the French first line of defence, French strategy has become more flexible, envisaging participation in a "forward battle". Whereas some years ago the shorter range forces were thought of as a mere warning shot briefly preceding strategic reprisal for violation of French territory, French spokesmen now contemplate the possibility of participation in a tactical nuclear battle. The transition is not complete, however, and the shorter range forces are often referred to as "pre-strategic" weapons.

One of Robert McNamara's reasons for deploring small national nuclear forces was scepticism about their ability to survive and execute a retaliatory mission. There certainly are severe problems for a small nuclear power facing a big one. SSBN technology has so far provided an

French nuclear forces are on the verge of a very rapid expansion if the costs of projected programmes can be met. While some components of the force may be open to attrition by defences or by pre-emptive attack, the total power of the force poses a threat that must be taken very seriously.

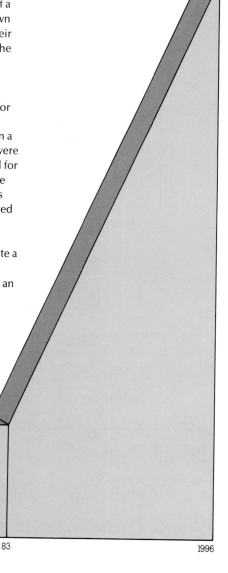

French strategic nuclear weapons 1963-1996

— 150

— 100

— 50

676
132 132
118 116
102
86
61
36 36 36
24
8
1

1963 64 65 66   69 1970 71   73 74   76   79 1980   83   1996

The French Pluton tactical nuclear missile is based in France and its range precludes targets beyond West Germany. The new Hades has a longer range said to relieve this embarrassment but, as the map shows, it does so only slightly. French tactical aircraft can reach most of East Germany if they can penetrate defences; whether the Mirage force could exploit the theoretical range shown here is doubtful, but the threat may still not be without deterrent effect.

apparently viable solution to pre-launch survival, but small numbers of boats can mean relatively few on station in crisis and consequent vulnerability to Soviet ASW. Elaborate precautions have to be taken to avoid trailing by hunter killers on leaving port. Should the Superpowers deploy ABM defences, the lesser forces would face serious penetration problems; both France and Britain have already spent considerable sums just to be confident of penetrating the relatively crude Galosh system around Moscow. As the demands on C^3I become greater, additional problems arise, especially if it is desired to be wholly independent of American facilities. Solving some of these problems is one of the major incentives for those who urge closer Franco-British collaboration in nuclear matters. One of the more commonly advocated initial steps is co-ordination of submarine patrols to sustain the maximum possible level of Franco-British force on firing station. As survivability in crisis is the essence of deterrence, however, even this apparently limited degree of mutual trust is actually quite demanding of political and strategic agreement.

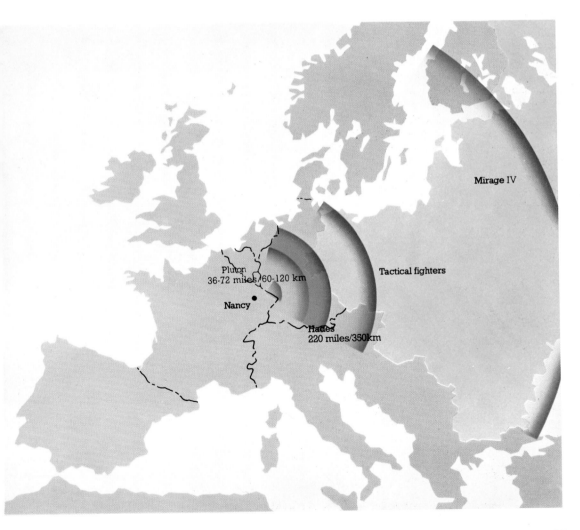

Mirage IV

Tactical fighters

Pluton
36-72 miles/60-120 km

Nancy

Hades
220 miles/350km

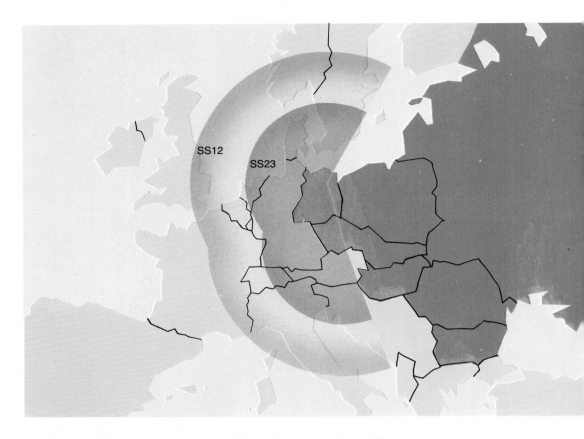

Anti Theatre Ballistic Missiles

Ballistic missiles are becoming increasingly important potential elements in theatre warfare. Both NATO and the Warsaw Pact have long deployed short range nuclear missiles, chiefly of US and Soviet origin, although the French have developed missiles of their own, the Pluton and the Hades. Until recently such missiles were relatively inaccurate and the fairly large warheads required to compensate made use difficult and dangerous, particularly as possible provocation to escalate to the strategic level. Nevertheless, until the Soviet Union began to admit that a war in Europe might just remain conventional, the typical Soviet picture of theatre war was of one beginning with the widespread use of nuclear missiles to secure a devastating early advantage.

Today much greater accuracy is possible and the Soviet Union has deployed a whole family of shorter range missiles from the SS21, at about 120 km range, through the SS23 at about 500 km and the SS22 or modified SS12 (Scaleboard) at about 1000 km range. These weapons may provide a capability to launch a more discriminatory nuclear attack to which NATO might be reluctant to respond in an unrestrained way. NATO's own arsenal of such weapons is limited to the French weapons and to the US Lance, about 120 km and Pershing I and II. To these may be added the GLCM but this, with Pershing II, is seen as a counterpoise to the 3000 km MIRVd SS20.

The map shows the range of the Soviet SS12 (modified) and SS23 missiles. Although regarded as only of medium or shorter range for theatre missiles they clearly provide coverage of a large part of Western Europe. There is speculation as to whether the accuracy is sufficient to permit a useful role with conventional warheads.

The Soviet SA12 (above) anti-aircraft missile has been provided with an anti-missile capability. The American Patriot (below) is a front-runner for modification to provide NATO with an anti-missile defence against such threats as the SS12. Such developments are a logical strategic as well as technological extension of air defence modernisation as ballistic missiles come to form part of the threat.

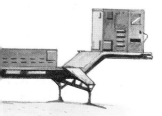

The accuracy of the more modern missiles opens up the possibility of achieving considerable results with conventional explosives for certain purposes. One of the most profitable might be the suppression of airfields with a consequent major impact on the land battle; ballistic missiles would have the advantage of sparing manned aircraft from attacking such highly defended targets. Chemical warheads might be particularly effective in impeding airfield operations.

The growing weight of the ballistic missile in theatre air warfare has naturally created interest in ABM defences for theatre use. In some respects this task is technologically easier than ABM for strategic weapons for, although warning times are less, re-entry speeds of theatre missiles are less, as is the capability to carry elaborate penetration aids. Moreover as theatre missiles are typically aimed at military targets, lower standards of effectiveness in the defence can still offer useful gains. The Soviet Union has already tested SA10 and 12 missiles in an anti-missile mode and the US Patriot air defence missile is widely regarded as adaptable to ABM use. Strictly speaking, ABM for theatre and tactical use escapes the ABM Treaty, which deals with strategic weapons, and some of the technology being developed for strategic ABM might find earlier application in theatre warfare. So far as NATO is concerned, however, there might be considerable European political reluctance to seem to drive a wedge into the ABM Treaty, and difficult questions arise as to who should pay. On the other hand, the somewhat irrational fear that a United States with SDI might retreat into a "Fortress America" could be reduced if Europe seemed to be acquiring its own protection.

Middle Eastern Conflict

The Middle East is one of the world's most turbulent political regions, one of the major concentrations of armaments and the scene of continuous warfare; it is as yet, however, a potential rather than an actual centre of nuclear activity.

A great many geopolitical factors combine to give the Middle East its strategic importance. It is an area of post-colonial territorial adjustment and the scene not merely of the pugnacious Arab-Israeli confrontation but of bitter sectarian disputes between Moslems. It is the source of much of the world's oil and while this looms less as a political issue since the end of the great energy panic, the continued flow of Gulf oil is a major strategic concern. It was this, combined with increased projection of Soviet power into the area and beyond, that led the United States to establish what was at first known as its Rapid Deployment Force. This takes on added relevance because of the geopolitical significance of the Middle East. The Suez Canal, less valuable than once, still symbolises the role of the area as a bridge between three continents; in the modern age, overflight becomes as strategically valuable as passage by sea.

Turkey, at once a Middle Eastern state and a member of NATO, demonstrates the interlocking of the two great European military blocs into the Middle Eastern arena. In scenarios for Soviet intervention in the Gulf area, Turkey looms large as the possible base for an American threat to Soviet flanks. Hitherto the Superpowers have shown great caution about direct confrontation but, on the other hand, President Nixon described the 1970 Jordanian crisis as the closest the world has come to a major war since 1945, and the 1973 Egyptian-Israeli war produced one of the highest states of alert the U S has ever adopted.

The amount of armament possessed by Middle Eastern states is very large as a result of local tensions, the wealth of the Arabs and the assistance rendered by the Superpowers, particularly by the United States to Israel. Israel is as yet the only power believed to possess either nuclear weapons or a hair-trigger option on them; Israeli skill is undoubted, and diversions of nuclear material suggest she has the wherewithal. Several Arab states have shown interest in getting nuclear weapons, President Gaddafi of Libya having allegedly tried to buy some from China. The most serious local programme was that of Iraq, impeded by the Israeli bombing of an almost completed reactor at Dimona in June 1981, one of the more dramatic implementations of a non-proliferation policy. Israel's own nuclear potential is presumably intended partly as insurance against Arab acquisition, partly to constitute a last-resort response to the failure of Israeli conventional defences, and partly to deter the Soviet Union from supporting the Arabs too far. Whether Israel has any thought of delivering a nuclear strike on the Soviet Union, or of seeming to be able to do so as a deterrent, is doubtful.

The other nuclear powers in the area are, of course, the Superpowers. For decades the US Sixth Fleet has been a permanent feature of the strategic scene; once part of flanking strike force against the Soviet Union itself, the Fleet is now primarily a factor in the regional balance but retains a residual strategic potential. SSBNs deployed to the Mediterranean form part of SACEUR's nuclear capability. Ever since the

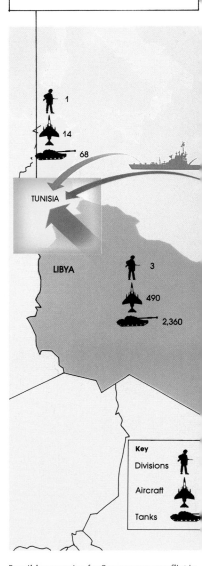

1 Libya attacks Tunisia. US supports Tunisia, USSR supports Libya.

Possible scenarios for Superpower conflict in the Middle East.

1950s the Soviet fleet has also had a permanent presence and this too includes nuclear elements. Their chief role is probably to neutralise the Sixth Fleet as a force on the flanks of a major European war, but embroilment in local conflict is always possible. Both Superpowers would doubtless try to avert the appearance of significant regional nuclear forces.

2 *Libya and Egypt go to war. USSR supports Libya, USA supports Egypt.*

3 *US strikes at terrorist bases in Syria and/or Lebanon. Syrian/US conflict breaks out. Soviet supports Syria.*

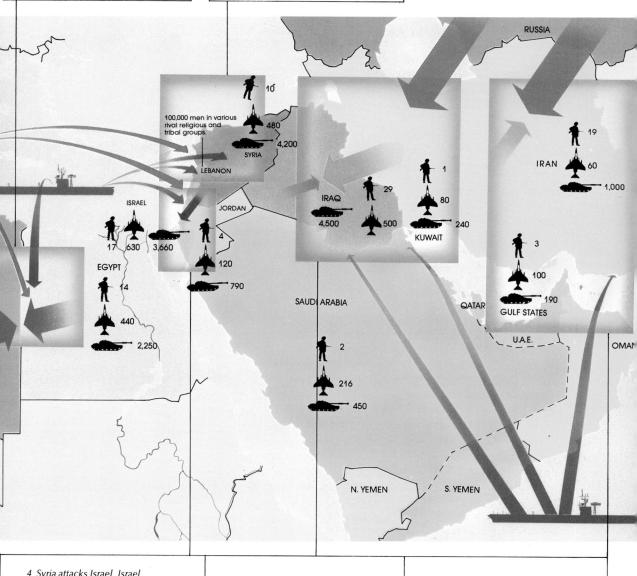

100,000 men in various rival religious and tribal groups.

LEBANON

SYRIA
10
480
4,200

ISRAEL
17 630 3,660

EGYPT
14
440
2,250

JORDAN
4
120
790

RUSSIA

IRAN
19
60
1,000

IRAQ
29
4,500 500

KUWAIT
1
80
240

GULF STATES
3
100
190

QATAR

U.A.E.

OMAN

SAUDI ARABIA
2
216
450

N. YEMEN

S. YEMEN

4 *Syria attacks Israel. Israel defeated. Nuclear weapons used by Israel. Soviets support Syria, US supports Israel. Or Israel defeats Syria. Syria supported by Soviets, US supports Israel.*

5 *Iran defeats Iraq. US moves to support Saudi Arabia and Gulf States. Soviets mobilize forces near Iran.*

6 *Soviet Union intervenes in Iran. US occupies southern Iran.*

Far Eastern Balance

East Asia is a heavily armed area of the world and one that has been the scene of the most severe and prolonged wars since 1945, including two conflicts, Korea and Vietnam, directly involving the United States and deeply influencing its strategy, diplomacy and domestic politics.

China, potentially the greatest power but still economically weak, maintains large but generally poorly equipped forces and is currently giving them lower priority in expenditure. Japan has limited its defence spending to about 1% of GNP, but this is a very large absolute sum of money. There has recently been some sign of less inhibition about military policy. Both Superpowers are major factors in the Asian strategic scene: the Soviet Union inevitably so by reason of geography; the United States continuing a policy of power projection in the area dating back over a century.

The area contains one full indigenous nuclear power, China, one with proven capability, India, and a leading candidate for proliferation, Pakistan. Japan clearly has the capacity to go nuclear, but is inhibited both by its anti-military constitution and by a natural antipathy to nuclear weapons born of its experience as the world's only victim of nuclear bombing. The latter emotion could obviously prove an unstable factor if the Japanese ever came to believe that the best protection against nuclear attack was a national nuclear force.

China scoffed at nuclear weapons before it had them — the "paper tiger" — but has shown great respect since acquiring them, including co-operation with other nuclear powers in discouraging proliferation elsewhere. China's belief that the Soviet Union failed to extend adequate nuclear protection to it in its conflicts with the United States in the 1950s was a factor in the Sino-Soviet split. China, in border dispute with the Soviet Union, as a neighbouring very large power a natural rival, sees its nuclear force as a guarantee against Soviet attack, especially nuclear. The Soviet Union's security policy seems to be to dedicate a large IRBM force as well as presumably part of its strategic force to Chinese targets, in order to neutralise China's nuclear forces, and to offset Chinese conventional forces by maintaining technologically superior forces on the border capable of launching powerful inroads into China. Doubtless if it came to war, the Soviet Union would try to avoid being drawn into China's vast territory.

Other sources of conflict exist in South East Asia and between India and Pakistan. Both Superpowers have a military presence. Since acquiring bases in Vietnam the Soviet Union has emulated on a small scale the traditional American policy of forward naval basing. In recent years the Soviet presence has increased and the once elaborate American treaty and alliance network has eroded, the latest manifestation being New Zealand's anti-nuclear policy. The record suggests, however, that the Superpowers will take great care not to collide directly with each other.

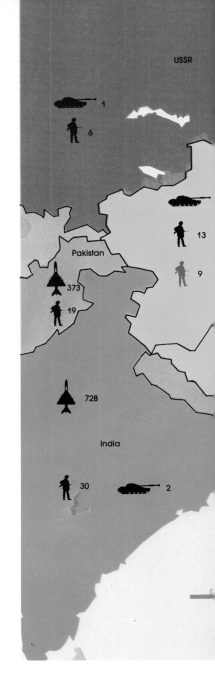

East Asia presents one of the world's more complex military balances. While the armed forces of the area are large there are vast variations in quality so that the data presented here must be interpreted with caution.

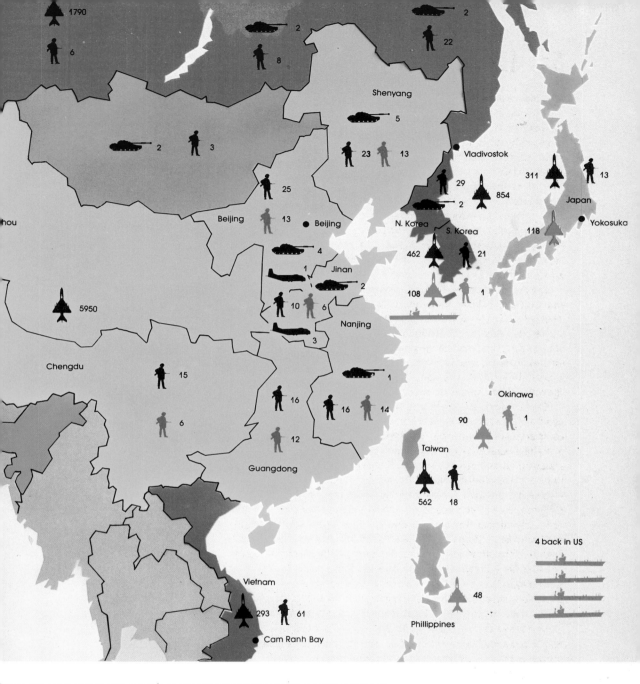
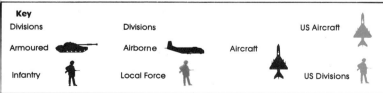

Fission / Fusion

The energy of a nuclear explosion is released when atomic nuclei split or fuse. An atom consists of a nucleus and electrons which orbit the nucleus. In chemical reactions, electrons are rearranged. In nuclear explosions the protons and neutrons which make up the nucleus itself are rearranged. Bombarding very heavy atoms, which have many protons and neutrons, with other neutrons may produce fission, creating new atoms and releasing spare neutrons to continue bombardment in a "chain reaction". The only natural element susceptible to this process is the isotope of uranium U235 which constitutes about 0.7% of natural uranium of which the rest is U238. U238 has 92 protons and 146 neutrons; U235 92 protons and 143 neutrons. Under controlled bombardment in a reactor, uranium can produce an artificial element, plutonium (P239), which is also capable of sustaining chain reactions. At the farther end of the spectrum the very light nuclei of some forms of hydrogen, containing only a few particles, may fuse if subjected to very high temperatures; in weapons, this "thermonuclear" reaction is induced by using a small fission device as a trigger. The two most commonly used isotopes of hydrogen are deuterium and tritium.

A chain reaction requires a critical mass of fissionable material so that sufficient neutrons collide with enough atoms. Otherwise the reaction "fizzles". But to assemble a critical mass runs the risk of spontaneous explosion by stray neutrons. Weapon design consequently involves assembling the components of a critical mass separately — most commonly in a hollow sphere, less frequently in an assembly where a cylinder can be inserted in a tube. To detonate the weapon conventional explosive either fires the cylinder into the tube ("gun" assembly) or the sphere is "imploded" by carefully machined lenses of HE placed around it. The absolutely precise and instantaneous compression of the material into a "supercritical" mass is essential to obtain a good explosive yield. Possible spontaneous explosions set physical limits on the safe size of fission weapons: fusion weapons can, however, be made almost as large as desired for the quantities of deuterium, usually employed as lithium deuteride, are not themselves dangerous.

Making a nuclear warhead therefore requires either the irradiation of U238 to produce plutonium, which is then chemically separated, or separating U235 from U238 by one of several difficult physical processes which make use of their different masses. The material, which is highly dangerous by reason of radiation or toxicity, must be very precisely machined into the appropriate shapes. This is, however, only the beginning, for very high skills are needed to prepare the HE components and to install fuses that ensure even detonation at the right time, at least if the weapon is to make efficient use of the full potential of the expensive fissile material.

A chain reaction requires a mass of fissile material sufficiently large and dense that enough released neutrons collide with remaining atoms of fissile material. The illustration shows a neutron colliding with an atom of U235, causing it to split and releasing further neutrons to bombard further atoms; some fission fragments escape, others may react with U238 to create plutonium.

Nuclear explosions release their energy in several different ways: explosive blast (if the explosion is in the atmosphere), similar to that produced by chemical explosions but with some special effects when on the largest scales (this is usually about 50% of total released energy); direct nuclear radiation of limited range, though it may induce long lasting radioactivity in particles of matter, hence "fall-out"; thermal radiation (about 35% of the total); and pulses of electrical and magnetic energy, electromagnetic pulse or EMP. Complete fission of a pound of uranium or plutonium releases energy equal to 8000 tons (8KT) of TNT.

The light element, hydrogen, exists in three forms: hydrogen, deuterium and tritium. Each has one proton but deuterium and tritium also have one and two neutrons respectively. At very high temperatures these atoms can be made to fuse; the fusion of all the nuclei in a pound of deuterium releases roughly the energy of 26,000 tons of TNT. This process can also release neutrons of sufficient energy to cause fission in U238; a fusion weapon can thus be relatively cheaply enhanced by jacketing it with natural U238.

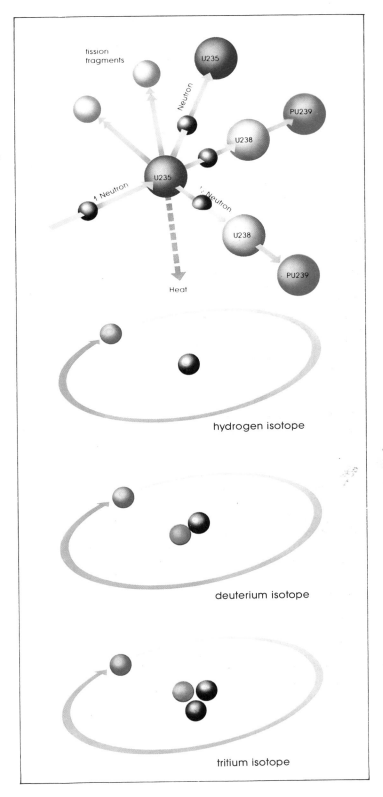

fission fragments

U235

Neutron

PU239

U238

U235

1 Neutron

Neutron

U238

PU239

Heat

hydrogen isotope

deuterium isotope

tritium isotope

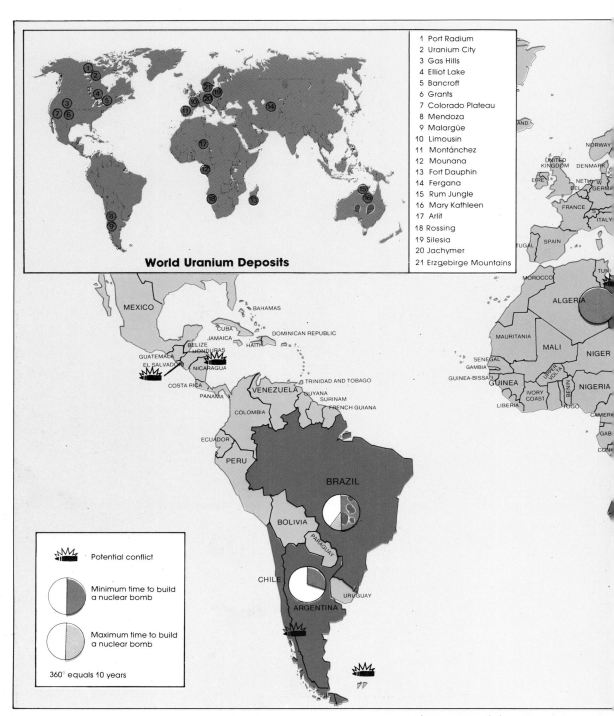

World Uranium Deposits

1 Port Radium
2 Uranium City
3 Gas Hills
4 Elliot Lake
5 Bancroft
6 Grants
7 Colorado Plateau
8 Mendoza
9 Malargüe
10 Limousin
11 Montánchez
12 Mounana
13 Fort Dauphin
14 Fergana
15 Rum Jungle
16 Mary Kathleen
17 Arlit
18 Rossing
19 Silesia
20 Jachymer
21 Erzgebirge Mountains

Potential conflict

Minimum time to build
a nuclear bomb

Maximum time to build
a nuclear bomb

360° equals 10 years

There are presently five nations with
declared nuclear force. In addition, many
believe that Israel has a covert supply of
weapons, at least close to assembly, and that
South Africa and Pakistan are well on the way
to acquiring all the necessary technology.
India has already exploded a nuclear
"device", but claims this was a peaceful
experiment. To create a weapon requires

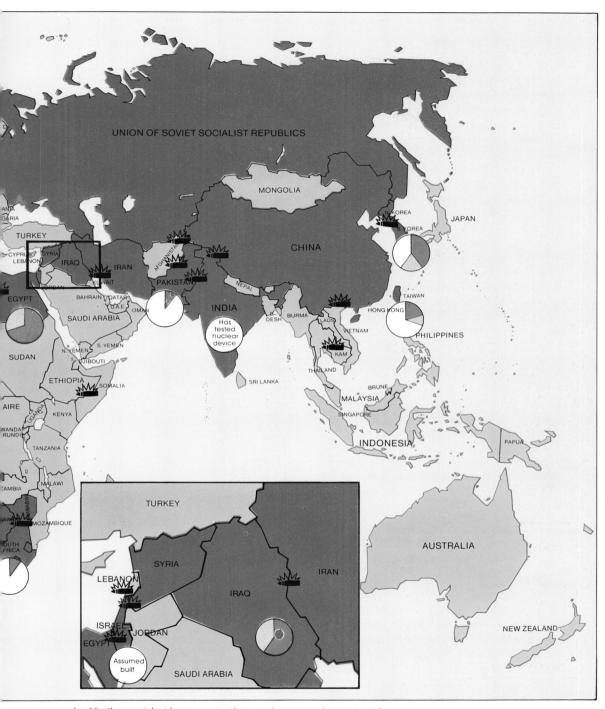

access to a supply of fissile material, either as crude uranium ore or as a more refined product, and the technology to process it and "weaponise" it with fuses, safety devices and so on in a deliverable package. The technical knowledge is now widely disseminated, but supplies of material and of the more sophisticated components are both difficult and expensive to obtain. The significance of any particular instance of nuclear proliferation depends on the identity of the state acquiring it and the strategic situation in which it finds itself: if, for instance, it is embroiled in endemic conflict. Any instance of proliferation may, however, have a general influence on the overall pace of the process.

Proliferation

To create a fully self-sufficient nuclear industry requires considerable expense and technological capacity, and the good fortune to have access to the raw material. The existing nuclear powers persuaded most other states to sign a Non-Proliferation Treaty (NPT) in 1969 whereby the non-nuclear states pledged not to acquire nuclear weapons and the nuclear states promised not to help them and also to work toward nuclear disarmament among themselves. Several significant possible nuclear powers refused to sign. Moreover the NPT has a double edge, for the nuclear powers promised to help other states develop nuclear energy for peaceful purposes, chiefly the generation of electrical power. Although the material for such programmes is supplied under safeguards, these are not perfect. More important, perhaps, the spread of civilian nuclear technology has disseminated a high degree of technological knowledge and capability far and wide throughout the world. While the nuclear powers have been united across political and ideological divides in trying to curb the spread of weapons, political desires to win favour with nations and commercial seeking for profit and export markets often gives great leverage to states seeking at least to acquire an "option" on nuclear weapons.

The tables opposite and overleaf indicate the progress of some of the most potent "candidate" nuclear powers.

Given the spread of nuclear technology, it is perhaps surprising that more proliferation has not taken place; two or three decades ago confident predictions were made of at least a couple of dozen nuclear powers by 1990.

The explanation lies in the balance of incentives rather than the physical difficulties. To acquire nuclear weapons may confer great military power and considerable prestige. But in a world where many powers — and much public opinion — condemns proliferation, there would also be much opprobrium. A main function of the NPT is to increase this.

As to security, a would-be acquirer of nuclear weapons has to consider disadvantages. His enemies may acquire nuclear weapons also under the stimulus of fear before he has achieved his own strategic purposes; a usable nuclear force as distinct from a single explosive device is not built overnight. The would-be nuclear power may have allies, perhaps nuclear-weapon states, who may abandon him. His enemies may have nuclear allies who can threaten retaliation on their behalf. All in all the equation is a complicated one, and many possible nuclear states seem to have decided that to be poised on the edge of nuclear power may be politically more effective than actual acquisition.

Thus even Israel, widely believed to have built or virtually built nuclear weapons, remains quiet on the subject. The nuclear powers of the future may not go through the open process of testing and announcing nuclear states pursued by the original five. Any new overt acquisition of weapons could, however, set off a limited or a general effort to follow.

This diagram and that on the following pages indicates the wide dispersal of nuclear knowledge and capability. Only a minority of leading participants in nuclear engineering have proceeded to acquire weapons, but all have major incentives to exploit their capability commercially and this provides a major driving force to disseminate capability. The diagram overleaf indicates the amount of that capability in the hands of a number of nations in political circumstances that make acquisition of nuclear weapons a possibly attractive option. Two or three of these are already in either overt (India) or covert (Israel) virtual possession of a weapon-capability.

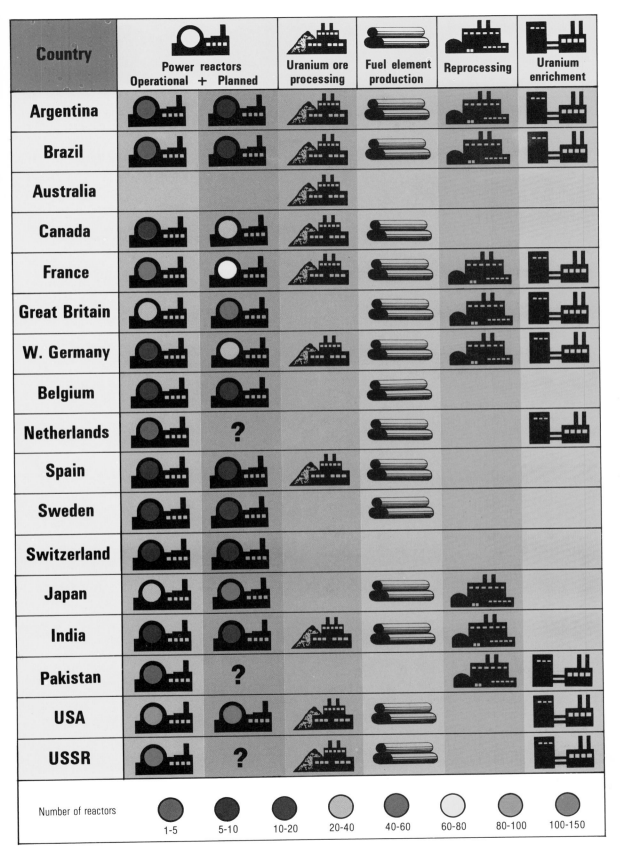

Country	Power reactors Operational + Planned		Uranium ore processing	Fuel element production	Reprocessing	Uranium enrichment
Argentina	⬤	⬤	⛰	▤	⬤	⬛
Brazil	⬤	⬤	⛰	▤	⬤	⬛
Australia			⛰			
Canada	⬤	◯	⛰	▤		
France	⬤	◯	⛰	▤	⬛	⬛
Great Britain	◯	⬤		▤	⬛	⬛
W. Germany	⬤	◯	⛰	▤	⬛	⬛
Belgium	⬤	⬤		▤		
Netherlands	⬤	?		▤		⬛
Spain	⬤	⬤	⛰	▤		
Sweden	⬤	⬤		▤		
Switzerland	⬤	⬤				
Japan	◯	⬤		▤	⬛	
India	⬤	⬤	⛰	▤	⬛	
Pakistan	⬤	?			⬛	⬛
USA	⬤	⬤	⛰	▤		⬛
USSR	⬤	?	⛰	▤		⬛

Number of reactors

1-5 5-10 10-20 20-40 40-60 60-80 80-100 100-150

85

	Non-Proliferation Treaty status	nuclear co-operation agreements	uranium reserves	research reactors
Argentina	non-member	Bolivia, Canada, Colombia, Ecuador, India, Italy, Paraguay, Peru, USA	23,000 tons assured & 39,000 more tons estimated	six
Brazil	non-member	Iraq, Italy, USA, Venezuela, West Germany	163,000 tons	three
Egypt	signed and ratified	USA, Egypt	5,000 tons	one
India	non-member	Argentina, Bangladesh, Belgium, Czechoslovakia, Denmark, East Germany, France, Hungary, Iraq, Philippines, Romania, Spain, USA, USSR, West Germany	42,500 tons	six
Iraq	signed and ratified	Brazil, France, India, USSR	none	two – one destroyed in Israeli air attack
Israel	non-member	USA, South Africa	30,000-60,000 tons	two
Libya	signed and ratified	Argentina, Pakistan, USSR	exploration only	one
Pakistan	non-member	France, Libya, UK	20,000 tons	one
South Africa	non-member	France, USA, Israel	448,000 tons	two
South Korea	signed and ratified	Canada, France, USA	10,000 tons	three
Taiwan	signed and ratified expelled from IAEA in 1972	USA	none	six

power-generation reactors	sensitive technologies			trained personnel	minimum time to build a bomb
	enrichment	reprocessing	heavy-water plants		
three in operation & three planned	minor capability	one under construction	two plants	very good	3 years
three in operation & six planned	three plants	two plants	none	moderate	3-6 years
eight planned	none	laboratory facility	none	poor	7-10 years
seven in operation & seven planned	none	three plants	seven plants	excellent	has tested nuclear device
none	none	one plant	none	some	6-10 years
none	one plant	one plant	one plant	excellent	assumed none
one planned	none	none	none	very few	10 years
one in operation	two plants	three plants	two plants	excellent	few months-1 year
two in operation	two plants	none	none	excellent	under 1 year
five in operation & eight planned	none	none	none	excellent	4-6 years
six in operation & six planned	none	dismantled laboratory facility	none	excellent	3 years +

Nature of Reactors

Nuclear reactors use the heat from nuclear reactions to boil water and generate power. Some material is used to slow down the neutrons produced by the reaction and control them so that an explosion does not occur. This material is called a moderator; in a light water reactor (LWR) the moderator is ordinary water; heavy water reactors use water containing a much higher proportion of deuterium than ordinary water. In some light water reactors the water around the fuel rods boils; in others the inner circuit is prevented from boiling by being under pressure — hence a "pressurised water reactor" or PWR — and this super-heated water boils a secondary circuit for power generation. Other reactors use graphite as a moderator and gas to take heat from the fuel; the British advanced gas-cooled reactor (AGR) uses highly enriched uranium as fuel whereas earlier reactors used natural uranium. A fourth experimental reactor is the "fast-breeder", in which the fuel is plutonium — frowned upon by foes of proliferation — the neutrons are not slowed down by a moderator and surrounding U238 can be radiated to produce more plutonium — hence "breeder". The coolant for the greater heat generated by this process is a liquid metal, usually sodium.

The process of using a reactor to produce plutonium is also that employed to acquire it for use in weapons. In practice it is more efficient to operate special reactors to produce weapon-grade material, but the process can be combined with the generation of power; this can substantially affect the economics of either activity.

The used reactor rods contain a variety of material, much of it highly dangerous. If weapon grade plutonium is required it must be removed by chemical processing. In any case there is a major problem of what to do with the spent fuel which represents a serious hazard which, while it diminishes quickly, retains some dangerous characteristics that can last for centuries. While there is no alternative to storing this material somewhere, reprocessing can reduce the mass requiring the most careful and prolonged custody. Nuclear waste could itself be used as an indiscriminate weapon and a commonly raised nightmare is its exploitation by terrorists. This possibility is only one complicating the expensive and politically sensitive task of transporting, handling and storing the by-products of reactors.

A simplified diagram depicts the steel pressure vessel of a reactor containing a graphite core as a moderator with fuel and rods inserted. The whole is surrounded by a concrete container to prevent the escape of radiation in the event of mishap. Computers control the insertion and removal of the rods to sustain the correct reactions. Coolant water is pumped through to extract heat used for steam generators.

Pressurised water reactors are the most widely disseminated power generating reactors and are also used for ship-propulsion; the self-contained process requiring only rare refuelling makes it particularly valuable in submarines.

Miscalculation or technical failure can give rise to excessive release of energy and over-heating. Although many safeguards are built in, of which perhaps the most reliable are truly massive pressure vessels and containment chambers, there have been one or two serious mishaps, and at Chernobyl, with the rupture of the pressure vessel, one of the worst fears was realised and in the absence of a secondary containment chamber a major release of radiation occurred.

Nevertheless, the nuclear reactor is now ubiquitous and with it a high degree of knowledge relevant to the military use of nuclear energy.

Nuclear reactor

thick concrete —

steel container —

control rods —

Fuel rods —

moderator —

coolant —

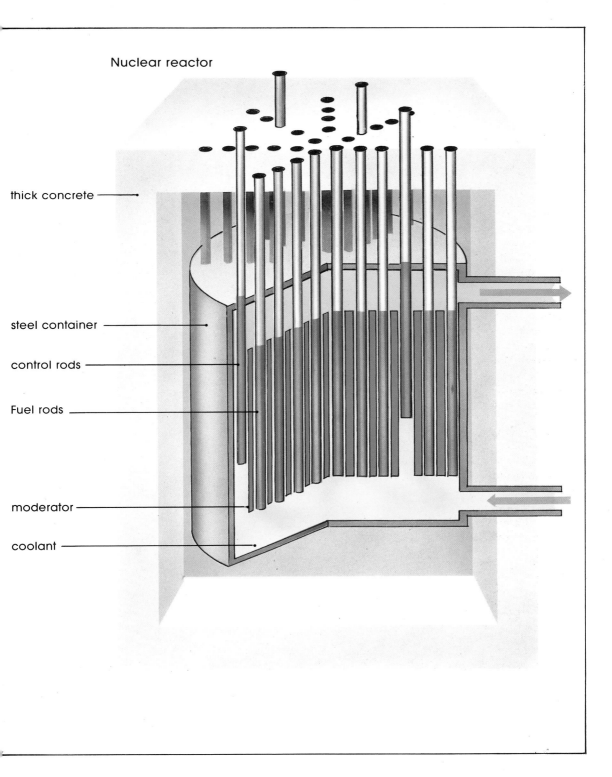

1 Soviet forces from Afghanistan cross Pakistan to attack Afghan camps.

2 Widespread rioting breaks out in Kashmir requiring Indian military intervention.

3 Indian forces pursue refugees/rebels over border into Pakistan.

5 Indian armour backed by infantry and artillery support thrusts into Pakistan.

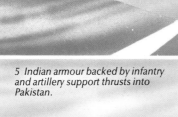

6 Conflict escalates and Indian numerical superiority takes its toll on Pakistan forces.

7 A crisis meeting of the Pakistan high command deliberates over the prospect of using nuclear weapons.

4 Indian troops attempt to close Kashmir border with Pakistan. Clashes occur.

8 Pakistan might see a nuclear pre-emptive strike as the only course left open.

Third World Conflict

The proliferation of nuclear weapons may perhaps increase the likelihood of nuclear war merely by raising the statistical probability. What more precisely concerns those who worry about proliferation is that it might place nuclear weapons in the hands of states that are embroiled in active conflicts — this would be one of the most rational motives for acquisition — and that those conflicts may not be embraced in the network of mutual deterrence that exists between the Soviet Union and its opponents. The very process of proliferation itself might be a major exacerbation of existing tension. Moreover a fledgling nuclear force might not be equipped with the safety devices and the control mechanisms gradually installed by the longer established nuclear powers. It is also possible that new nuclear powers would be unstable in their domestic politics; in that case the nuclear force might become a prize or weapon in internal political struggles.

A particular category of "candidate" state close to a nuclear power is the unflatteringly labelled "pariah" state, one like Israel, Taiwan or South Africa, which suffers political isolation from its neighbours and is sometimes regarded askance on a wider scale. The temptation to see nuclear weapons as an ultimate guarantee of security is obvious, as is the possibility that the occasion for use might arise.

In many discussions of nuclear diplomacy and politics, possible patterns of warfare are discussed without any plausible speculation as to what the occasion of a nuclear war would be. Wars are usually about something serious. In the Third World, conflicts serious enough for war are well proved to exist in profusion. The injection of nuclear weapons here could obviously be highly dangerous. If a government decides to use nuclear weapons it will doubtless be conscious of many disadvantages in doing so; it may happen, however, that bad though such an option may appear, the alternatives may seem worse.

A frequently considered scenario is set in the Indian subcontinent. India and Pakistan have strong military traditions, have sharp religious differences and a specific territorial dispute in Kashmir that has already caused wars. Pakistan has been dismembered once by India when Bangladesh was created.

It is possible to imagine a combination of tensions arising from the Soviet pressures on Pakistan over the Afghan war and Indian intervention in renewed Kashmiri trouble, perhaps caused by diversionary Pakistani political manoeuvres. A combination of pressure from India and its long-term associate the Soviet Union could lead to nervousness in Pakistan, precautionary military activity and a pre-emptive Indian attack, relying on conventional superiority and Soviet support. With the war going heavily against it, a Pakistani government whose domestic status was endangered might well regard the use of a nuclear weapon a reasonable gamble to secure what in NATO jargon would be called "war termination". In an area where nuclear weapons were relatively scarce this might not appear a decision for "assured destruction" in the Superpower sense. In turn, an India conscious that Pakistan had such an option might have been tempted to pre-empt. One of the Superpowers might consider issuing an ultimatum of support for any nuclear victim; it is even possible to imagine joint Superpower action, so grave would the issues have become.

Nuclear Terrorism

Terrorism has become an endemic feature of modern political life in many countries. Well established transnational links between terrorist groups have also made it an important aspect of international relations. Nuclear weapons being so powerful that their role even as instruments of national policy has been characterised as a "balance of terror" it is not surprising that there has been much speculation and anxiety about their falling into terrorist hands.

So far as is publicly known, there has been no instance of terrorists acquiring a nuclear weapon, although there have been many incidents of individuals and groups threatening to do so or claiming to have actually gained possession of nuclear material. There have also been numerous threats to sabotage nuclear facilities. For obvious reasons, national authorities keep such episodes as unpublicised as possible.

There seems little doubt that an authentic or apparently authentic terrorist threat to use a nuclear weapon or other form of nuclear material would cause immense alarm; nuclear phenomena, like poisons, engender particular anxiety, and several books and movies have been devoted to this theme. The fact that no such episode has occurred testifies, however, to the difficulties besetting the would-be perpetrators.

In the first place, such material would be very difficult to acquire. Military weapons are naturally closely guarded and all the facilities to do so are readily available. Close security is also maintained over civil nuclear installations and many countries have special para-military forces to do so. Moreover, the very dangerousness of radioactive material poses great hazards for any who might tamper with it and even suicidal terrorists would face practical difficulties in keeping the material safe and effective; once the worst had happened the political leverage would have dissipated. Finally, experts on terrorism question whether a mass threat would in fact serve many terrorist purposes, for terrorists usually rely on an element of political support for their cause in the target community. Even so, the success of terrorism in achieving political goals is not impressive, despite the incidental fear and inconvenience caused.

Nevertheless, extreme safeguards are taken with nuclear facilities, especially atomic weapons. In addition to careful custody, technology can be employed. Thus many modern nuclear weapons contain tamper-proof devices, usually associated with those designed to prevent unauthorised military use. Such devices can ensure that the weapon would not yield a nuclear explosion, though it is more difficult to preclude the mere release of radioactive material. Transport vehicles are also fitted with elaborate security mechanisms, and many nuclear weapons are transported only by air. Terrorism still remains a serious worry, however, complicated by the fact that considerable public anxiety and probable consequent political embarrassment could be engendered merely by a plausible bluff; nuclear matters are so shrouded in secrecy that proving something had *not* happened could be far from easy.

1 Terrorists seize train transporting nuclear waste.

2 Terrorists threaten to blow up containers above major river unless demands are met.

3 Government mobilises special anti-nuclear terror unit.

4 Terrorists kill train crew to show determination.

5 Government agonises over action; summons foreign experts.

6 Terrorists prepare to blow up bridge.

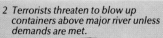

Effects of Nuclear Explosions

The explosion of a nuclear weapon gives rise to a variety of powerful phenomena. Some of these depend on the type of burst — e.g. atmospheric, low or high altitude, on the surface or below it — and selecting the appropriate mode of use is an important tactical consideration. This selection influences the interaction of the initial energy of the explosion with its environment and consequently the ratio between the forms in which the energy is transmitted, e.g. blast, shock, and thermal radiation. Weather conditions are also important: fog can limit thermal radiation, wind can distribute fall-out particles.

In a fission explosion, the components of the weapon rapidly rise to temperatures of several tens of millions degrees, equivalent to the centre of the sun; the temperatures of chemical explosions are at most some 5000°C. All the matter becomes gasified within the approximate volume of the original weapon; thus immense pressures are created. Within a millionth of a second, huge amounts of X-ray energy are released and absorbed by the atmosphere, forming a hot, luminous mass or fireball. Observers of early tests noted that a 1 MT fireball appeared several times brighter than the sun from over 50 miles (80 km) away. The fireball now rapidly grows and rises. In about a minute a 1 MT fireball rises over 4 miles (6.5 km); during this process gases condense again to form particles. If the weapon is close enough to the surface, the updraft will pull debris up into the radioactive cloud. This will be a mixture of debris, water from the atmosphere and fission products from the weapon itself. If even 1% of the energy from a 1 MT weapon is enabled by low altitude of the fireball to vaporise matter on the ground, some 4000 tons of material will be added to the cloud, leaving a crater. The equivalent pickup of water over the sea or lakes would be some 20,000 tons. This is the source of radioactive fall-out, distribution of which will then be determined by the direction and speed of wind. Early fall-out of visible particles is usually complete in 24 hours; this local fall-out is succeeded by delayed fall-out which may occur world wide.

Immediately after the explosion, a shock wave of compressed air moves rapidly out, travelling about 3 miles (4.8 km) in the first 10 seconds; in 50 seconds it travels 12 miles (19.3 km), still moving faster than sound. A secondary blast wave caused by reflection of the first is also very powerful. Where the two waves meet occur the highest "over-pressures"; after an explosion at 6,500 feet, a 1 MT bomb will produce this in a circle roughly 1.3 miles from the ground zero (i.e. the point directly under the explosion). At this point the over-pressure would be about 16 lbs. sq. in. or twice normal atmospheric pressure. Transient winds will reach velocities of hundreds of miles an hour.

The weapon also emits thermal radiation; Individuals may suffer burns up to 12 miles from a 1 MT weapon. In addition, various nuclear radiations occur. The fission process emits neutron and gamma rays; this is so-called prompt radiation, from the actual explosion. Further gamma and beta radiation emerges from the decay of radioactive particles. The fusion portion of the weapon produces chiefly neutrons.

All of the effects described here do severe damage to targets. The chief mechanisms of damage to buildings are blast and fire. Sudden

Diagram shows the destructive effect of a 1 MT airburst; the significant prompt effects are thermal radiation and blast. The radii from ground zero are only approximations; actual effects would vary considerably according to topography and meteorological conditions. Variations could also arise from the height of the burst.

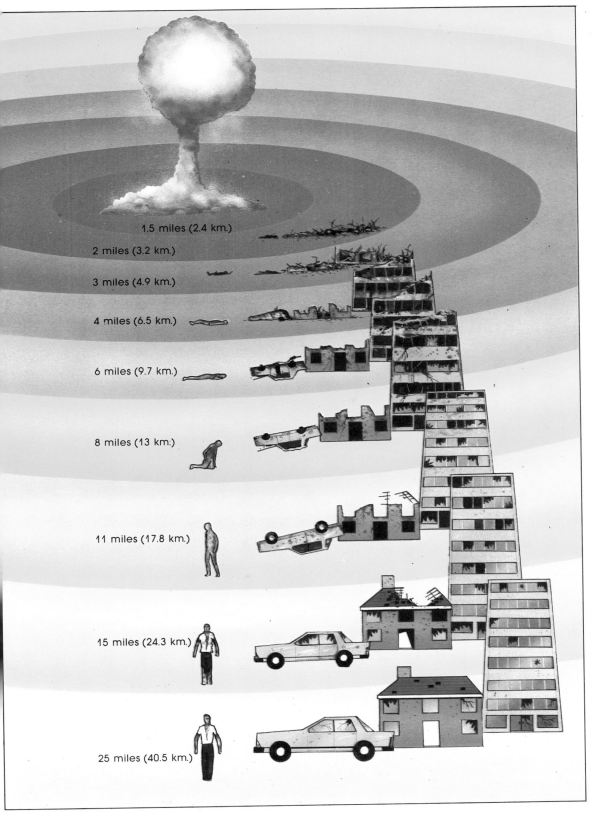

1.5 miles (2.4 km.)

2 miles (3.2 km.)

3 miles (4.9 km.)

4 miles (6.5 km.)

6 miles (9.7 km.)

8 miles (13 km.)

11 miles (17.8 km.)

15 miles (24.3 km.)

25 miles (40.5 km.)

over-pressures crush objects, while the dynamic over-pressures of wind also knock them down. The over-pressure from 1 MT at 4 miles will exceed 5 lbs. per sq. in. (psi) exerting a force of some 180 tons on the wall of an average sized house. People are usually injured not by this static over-pressure, but by being hurled about by the winds or crushed by the falling buildings.

Thermal radiation will cause fires, which will also arise from blast damage to sources of ignition. These effects are highly unpredictable; estimates suggest that at the 2 psi point about 10% of all buildings would ignite; this could lead to fire storms and conflagrations of the type experienced in World War II. Much depends on terrain and on the type of construction used for building in the target area. People will also be killed by prompt nuclear radiation and by fall-out.

Not a likely source of casualties, but important for military and other purposes, is the electromagnetic pulse (EMP) produced by nuclear explosions which may produce destructive or damaging effects in electrical equipment, or may trigger safety devices requiring considerable labour to reverse.

If nuclear weapons are used by NATO on the European battlefield, steps would have to be taken to avoid populated areas or to evacuate them. Friendly troops would need protection which could be prepared if NATO had the initiative. Standard NBC (Nuclear, Biological, Chemical) protection suits provide no shelter from prompt radiation but are of some use to protect from fall-out. Even with all possible precautions, nuclear weapons could only be used sparingly and in suitable locations if large civilian casualties are to be avoided. Enemy troops would do their best to exploit this by "city hugging" and getting rapidly into close proximity to friendly forces.

Enhanced Radiation Weapons

The early lead which the United States and NATO enjoyed over the Soviet Union in nuclear weapons began a process whereby the Western alliance has repeatedly sought ways in which nuclear weapons could provide a cheap and effective counter balance to the large conventional military power of the Soviet Union. Massive retaliation was the most extreme form of this and NATO's doctrine of "flexible response", whereby there would theoretically be graduated recourse to nuclear weapons if conventional defences failed, remains alliance policy.

Ever since a mere ill-defined threat of nuclear war came to appear a self-defeating strategy and an ineffective deterrent, once the Soviet Union had nuclear weapons of its own, efforts have been made to diversify NATO strategy. An early idea was the use of smaller nuclear weapons on the battlefield, to affect the course of the war by supplementing conventional firepower, rather than to threaten cities.

At first, in the mid-1950s, it was hoped the U S still possessed a big advantage over the Soviet Union in the provision of weapons for this purpose. Even before this ceased to be true, serious objections to the strategy arose. These chiefly concerned the effects it would have on friendly troops and especially civilians. War games suggested that millions of Germans would be killed in a European war by the "collateral" effect of NATO weapons. To this devastation would have to be added the effects of Soviet weapons presumably used in response. Even from a strictly military perspective it began to seem almost impossible to retain control over armies shattered by nuclear weapons.

A second wave of interest in "tactical" or "theatre" nuclear weapons arose in the 1970s when improved accuracy suggested the possibility of using much smaller warheads. One major difficulty had hitherto been that military targets such as dispersed tank regiments are quite resistant even to nuclear attack

Right: A depiction of the increased proportion of prompt radiation effect of an enhanced radiation weapon (ERW) or "neutron bomb" to the effect of blast. The main advantage in usability is to reduce the area of less predictable blast effect around that of certain radiation kill; but it is of course still necessary to consider the fate of friendly civilians and troops within the range of lethal effects.

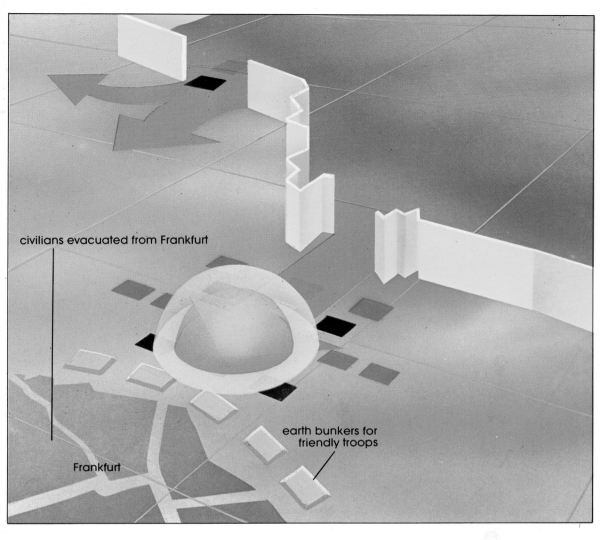

civilians evacuated from Frankfurt

earth bunkers for
friendly troops

Frankfurt

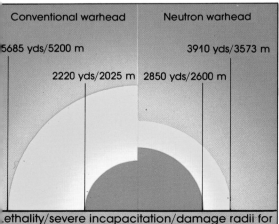

Conventional warhead	Neutron warhead
5685 yds/5200 m	3910 yds/3573 m
2220 yds/2025 m	2850 yds/2600 m

Lethality/severe incapacitation/damage radii for small tactical fission weapons (nominal yield 1 kt air-bursting at 3280 ft/1000m) depicted to scale.

radius of lethality
(blast & radiation)

radius of damage
(blast & heat)

The interest in more "usable" nuclear weapons stimulated considerable attention to "enhanced radiation weapons" which were designed, chiefly by reducing the fission component to a minimum, so that the weapon was effectively a small H-bomb, and a much greater proportion of its energy would be released as prompt radiation (hence "neutron bomb") and less as heat and blast than with a fisson weapon. The area of collateral damage is thus considerably reduced in relation to useful military effect.

While such weapons are probably among the most useful if nuclear weapons are to be used on the battlefield at all, they do no more than reduce the problem of collateral damage or of battle control. Fear that such weapons made nuclear "war fighting" more likely led NATO to abandon plans to deploy ERW in 1978. France, however, is believed to be developing such a weapon for its own forces.

Effects of Radiation

The effects of radiation on living organisms are still not fully understood; where it was once generally believed there were "thresholds" below which harm was negligible, the model now preferred is one of a continuum.

Of the four main types of radiation, alpha and beta particles with little capability to penetrate skin are unlikely to present a major hazard unless ingested as fall-out. Gamma rays, however, are like highly energetic X-rays; capable of penetrating inches of concrete, they easily invade the body. Neutrons also penetrate freely.

Radiation is omnipresent in our environment, but close exposure to the effects of nuclear explosions would give immensely higher, untypical doses. Radiation affects the electrical charges of components of the body; by creating positive or negative ions (hence "ionising radiation") radiation can intensify the activity of cells and accelerate their multiplication; thus areas of the body already typically active in self-replication are particularly vulnerable sites for radiation damage. This may manifest itself early as nausea, vomiting and diarrhoea. For lesser doses, effects may appear after two or three weeks as hair loss and haemorrhages. Damage to bone marrow may produce anaemia with consequent vulnerability to infections. This may also be induced by damage to lymph nodes. Longer term effects in those who survive such prompt damage are various forms of cancer and leukaemia. Obviously the effect of radiation will compound injury suffered from blast or burning. Clearly no-one can be killed more than once, however, and studies suggest synergistic effects are not very important for prompt deaths and affect chiefly the longer term consequences.

Indeed it is probable that although nuclear radiation of more than 50 "rem" (i.e. the absorption of 50 roentgen) would produce some prompt medical consequences, this is not likely to be exceeded more than two miles from ground zero of a 1 MT surface explosion and most people within that radius would be killed by blast. In areas further away, the vulnerability to such phenomena as thermal radiation will depend on circumstances, e.g. in summer more people are likely to be in the open air, but this again will vary according to whether there has been significant warning, whether shelters are available and so on. The availability of long term shelter facilities can have dramatic effects on the delayed consequences of fall-out.

Many of the effects of lesser exposures can be mitigated by medical treatment. In a major nuclear catastrophe, however, medical services would inevitably be greatly degraded; indeed, further health hazards would arise from the destruction of medical facilities and public health measures. Most hospital beds are in central urban areas, as are often the key utility services.

The rate at which cells naturally multiply in the body is a major determinant of vulnerability to radiation damage. The diagram locates and rates the systems of the body in order of highest activity and hence of increased sensitivity.

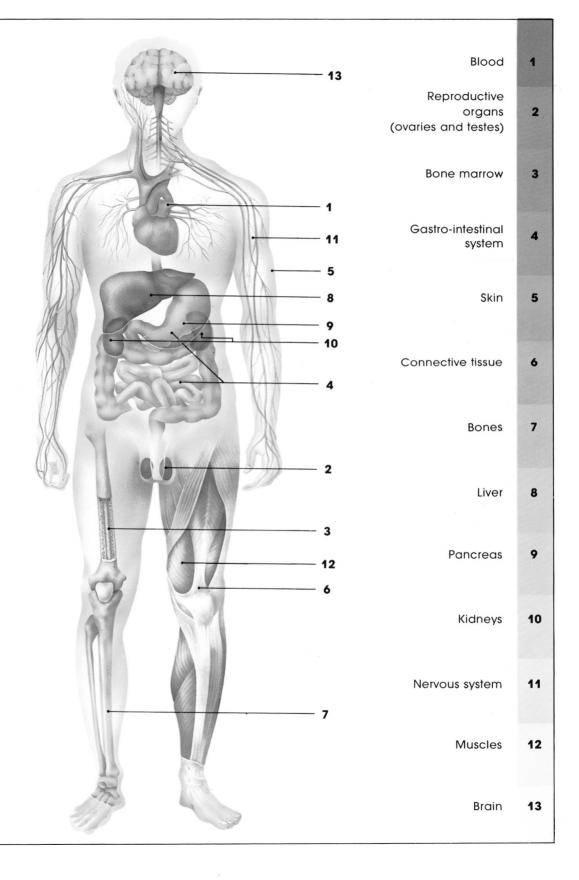

Blood	**1**
Reproductive organs (ovaries and testes)	**2**
Bone marrow	**3**
Gastro-intestinal system	**4**
Skin	**5**
Connective tissue	**6**
Bones	**7**
Liver	**8**
Pancreas	**9**
Kidneys	**10**
Nervous system	**11**
Muscles	**12**
Brain	**13**

Civil Defence

In World War II Civil Defence was ubiquitous in mitigating the consequences of strategic bombing. Once the power of thermonuclear weapons was fully appreciated, however, and the common image of nuclear warfare became one of mutual assured destruction, the task of civil defence came to be widely regarded as hopeless, at least in Western nations. This idea has proved persistent even though there have been recurrent official efforts to demonstrate that even in the nuclear age, civil defence could bring about very large reductions in casualties, particularly those that would otherwise be suffered from fall-out beyond the immediate target areas of devastation. Western governments have been erratic and reluctant in pressing the case for civil defence; two probable reasons for this are the preference of the military for expenditure on the armed forces themselves, and political nervousness about making the possibility of nuclear war seem real or even imminent.

In the Soviet Union, by contrast, there has always officially been a large scale civil defence system and although expert opinions vary as to how seriously and efficiently it is actually pursued, there seems no doubt that the programme is much more substantial than anything comparable in the West. The Soviet Union has also laid more stress than Western nations, at least until recently, on preserving not merely the national military command authorities but the whole network of political power and control.

Quite apart from the humanitarian values to be promoted by civil defence, strategists tend to emphasise the political leverage and credibility a high standard of preparation could confer on nuclear powers in a crisis of mutual deterrence; without some such preparations, it is suggested, deterrent threats would lack credibility. When the role of civil defence in crisis is considered, some important questions arise about the effect on "crisis stability"; would evacuation of population, for instance, seem to suggest preparation to launch an attack and thereby provoke pre-emption by the other side?

Throughout most of the nuclear age, the image of nuclear war as an all-out mutual onslaught has diminished the appeal of civil defence. The ideas of limited nuclear war now taken more seriously in strategic debate put this question in a new perspective. Quite clearly civil defence could be very effective if nuclear strikes were limited and defensive preparations could lend added credibility to the doctrine. The possibility that ABM defence may become a reality also suggests a context in which civil defence would have unmistakable advantages. A programme designed for such circumstances would also have value if predictions that a large war could remain conventional were vindicated.

The vulnerability of a nation to nuclear attack is greatly affected by the pattern in which its population is distributed. This will affect both the casualty rate per detonation and the scope for evacuation. The chart shows the wide variations in land area and population density for European countries. In practice much more detailed analysis is needed to determine the scope for sheltering and evacuation; population cannot be evacuated to a wilderness, so a large number of small or medium conurbations is preferable to a few large cities surrounded by open territory. The dispersion of population will also imply a spread of agricultural and industrial facilities which may greatly assist in post-attack recovery.

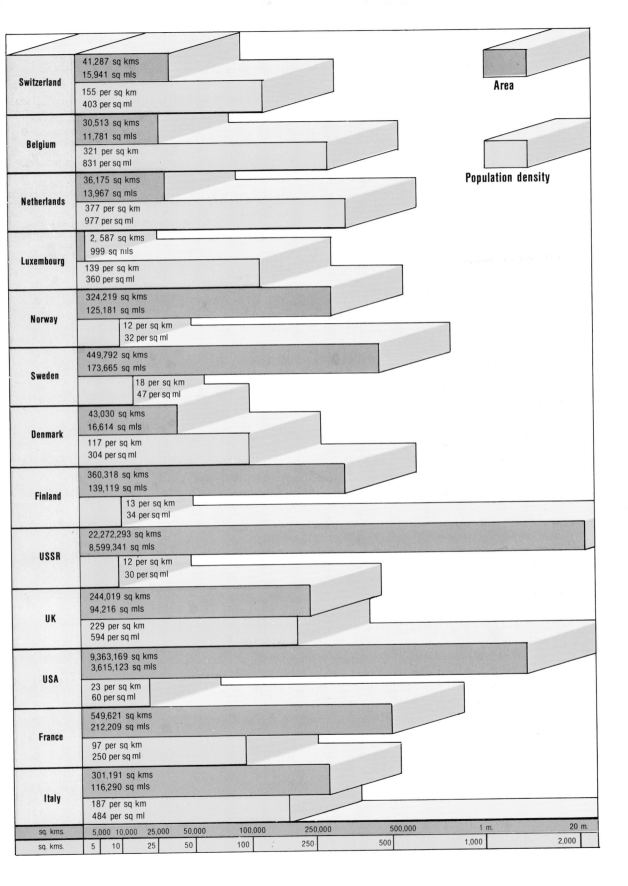

	Area	Population density
Switzerland	41,287 sq kms / 15,941 sq mls	155 per sq km / 403 per sq ml
Belgium	30,513 sq kms / 11,781 sq mls	321 per sq km / 831 per sq ml
Netherlands	36,175 sq kms / 13,967 sq mls	377 per sq km / 977 per sq ml
Luxembourg	2, 587 sq kms / 999 sq mls	139 per sq km / 360 per sq ml
Norway	324,219 sq kms / 125,181 sq mls	12 per sq km / 32 per sq ml
Sweden	449,792 sq kms / 173,665 sq mls	18 per sq km / 47 per sq ml
Denmark	43,030 sq kms / 16,614 sq mls	117 per sq km / 304 per sq ml
Finland	360,318 sq kms / 139,119 sq mls	13 per sq km / 34 per sq ml
USSR	22,272,293 sq kms / 8,599,341 sq mls	12 per sq km / 30 per sq ml
UK	244,019 sq kms / 94,216 sq mls	229 per sq km / 594 per sq ml
USA	9,363,169 sq kms / 3,615,123 sq mls	23 per sq km / 60 per sq ml
France	549,621 sq kms / 212,209 sq mls	97 per sq km / 250 per sq ml
Italy	301,191 sq kms / 116,290 sq mls	187 per sq km / 484 per sq ml

sq. kms.	5,000	10,000	25,000	50,000	100,000	250,000	500,000	1 m.	20 m.
sq. kms.	5	10	25	50	100	250	500	1,000	2,000

Strategic Arms Limitations

The modern history of theoretical discussion and even diplomatic negotiation about agreed disarmament goes back some 200 years, but the practical achievements have been few. Nevertheless, as the destructiveness of modern weapons has become exponentially greater, interest has grown as the flurry of negotiation between the two World Wars demonstrated. The degree of actual agreement reached, however, remained slight, patently contributed little to economy and failed to prevent a disastrous war. That experience does serve to show rather clearly that the motives for seeking disarmament agreements can be mixed and even contradictory; the reduction of expenditure on armaments may, for instance, actually increase the chances of war by adversely affecting the balance of power. With nuclear weapons making the prevention of war clearly the overriding aim, the goal in recent years has become that of "arms control" rather than simple *disarmament*, i.e. the hope is to reduce the chance of war and to limit its consequences if it does occur. Reducing military expenditure is a secondary consideration. But while this is the generally accepted theory, in political circles the simplistic assumption that any proposal to reduce armaments must have benign results is difficult to rebut even though in an age of deterrence it should be clear that the stability of the balance is all-important and that any piecemeal proposal should be judged in a comprehensive strategic context.

Nuclear weapons have undoubtedly created an entirely new climate for arms control because the common interest at least in averting a full scale nuclear war is unmistakable. Consequently, arms control has become a permanent issue in international and domestic politics. An unprecedented number of major agreements have actually been achieved as indicated on the accompanying tables. How far they go in dealing with the problems is debatable. As time passes it becomes clear that agreements alter in significance as technology, strategic thought and political relations evolve and that the agreements reached so far have in any case dealt with much easier issues than many important ones that remain.

The atmospheric Test Ban, for example, is an undoubted blessing as a public health measure and could be achieved because verification was easy. It has proved much less significant as an non-proliferation measure and almost irrelevant to the pace of technological evolution between the nuclear powers. The Non-Proliferation Treaty is a useful political adjunct to the whole network of disincentives to proliferation and if no more than that, is a constructive measure if not without drawbacks.

The centrepiece of arms control in the nuclear age has been the ABM Treaty and the SALT agreements. Today the former is under great strain, exemplified most clearly in pressure from advocates of the American Starwars programme but more generally put in question by technological change and failure to deal adequately with the problem of offensive weapons. Here SALT I put temporary limitations on the more easily counted weapons; SALT II failed to secure ratification in the United States because of deteriorating Soviet-American relations – thus

---

Strategic Arms Limitations

SALT 1

Treaty between the USA and the USSR on the limitation of anti-ballistic missile systems (ABM Treaty).
  Signed Moscow 26 May 1972: entered into force 3 October 1972

Protocol to the US-Soviet ABM Treaty.
  Signed Moscow 3 July 1974: entered into force 25 May 1976

Interim Agreement between the USA and the USSR on certain measures with respect to the limitation of strategic offensive arms.
  Signed Moscow 26 May 1972: entered into force 3 October 1972

Memorandum of Understanding between the USA and the USSR regarding the establishment of a Standing Consultative Commission on arms limitation.
  Signed Geneva 21 December 1972: entered into force 21 December 1972

SALT II

Treaty between the USA and the USSR on the limitation of strategic offensive arms (SALT II Treaty).
  Signed Vienna 18 June 1979: not in force

Protocol to the SALT II Treaty.
  Signed Vienna 18 June 1979: not in force

Joint Statement by the USA and the USSR of principles and basic guidelines for subsequent negotiations on the limitation of strategic arms.
  Signed Vienna 18 June 1979

---

illustrating the difficult "linkage" between arms control and wider issues — and was finally breached by a United States which believed it failed to curb competing Soviet military programmes — thus also illustrating the ease with which many arms control agreements prove merely to divert effort into unprohibited areas.

By the late 1980s the Reykjavik Soviet-American summit produced proposals to rectify some of these failings by really radical reductions in nuclear weapons. The subsequent alarm raised within NATO illustrated yet another difficulty; that nuclear weapons are closely linked to the rest of the balance of power and that efforts to stabilise relationships at one level may destabilise them elsewhere.

Arms control will remain a major feature of the strategic scene, certainly as a topic of negotiation, probably as a source of agreements. But there is little to suggest that any ultimate solutions or permanent resting places are available. The future seems likely, like the past, to revolve around two major problems. First, what is to be controlled?

Restrictions on nuclear weapon testing
Treaty banning nuclear weapon tests in the atmosphere, in outer space and under water (Partial Test Ban Treaty — PTBT).
Signed Moscow 5 August 1963: entered into force 10 October 1963
Treaty between the USA and the USSR on the limitation of underground nuclear weapon tests (Threshold Test Ban Treaty — TTBT).
Signed Moscow 3 July 1974: not in force
Treaty between the USA and the USSR on underground nuclear explosions for peaceful purposes (Peaceful Nuclear Explosions Treaty — PNET).
Signed Moscow & Washington 28 May 1976: not in force

Non-proliferation of nuclear weapons
Treaty on the non-proliferation of nuclear weapons (NPT).
Signed London, Moscow & Washington 1 July 1968: entered into force 5 March 1970
Convention on the physical protection of nuclear material.
Signed Vienna & New York 3 March 1980.
UN Security Council Resolution on security assurances to non-nuclear weapon states.
Adopted 19 June 1968

So far as nuclear weapons are concerned there are such alternative criteria as numbers — of what? delivery vehicles, warheads etc?; quality and size — how? by explicit limits, by restrictions on testing?; balances — equal in all categories or equivalent in strategic effect with "freedom to mix"?; whose weapons? — how long can the lesser nuclear powers stay out of the Superpower calculations? There are also the vexed questions of verification. The first SALT agreements limited readily observable items — launchers — and could rely on "national technical means" (NTM) of verification — chiefly satellites. Closer control to lower limits may require intrusive "on site" inspection and, even if agreed in principle, that could be difficult in practice. The scope for ingenuity is apparent; so is that for frustration and misunderstanding.

Nuclear Weapons – The Hardware

The nuclear scene today is marked by the sheer number of different types and classes of nuclear weapons performing a wide range of missions. It is further confused by the widespread use of acronyms which often seem unintelligible. Although most of the language of strategic studies is useful and logical, there is an increasing tendency to use some terms interchangeably and to make new distinctions as new problems emerge. Nuclear weapons can in fact be defined by range, by use and by type.

Intercontinental weapons are by definition ones that can link continents. Thus a Chinese missile that can hit the United States or the European areas of the USSR is intercontinental in range, while an SS20 missile in Asia that could only hit targets in Asia would not qualify. By and large this definition holds, and the term is most commonly used to describe weapons able to strike the territory of one Superpower from the territory or the nearby waters of another. The Intercontinental Ballistic Missile, known as the ICBM, is the most common use of the term.

Intermediate range weapons have ranges between 2400 and 6400 km (1490 and 4000 miles), midway between the intercontinental weapons and medium range weapons. Again the term is most commonly used to describe a ballistic missile. Thus a French S3 land based missile and a Soviet SS4 missile would both be described as Intermediate Range Ballistic Missiles: IRBM.

Medium range weapons have ranges between 800 and 2400 km (500 and 1500 miles) giving Medium Range Ballistic Missiles as MRBM.

Short range weapons include all those with ranges below 800km (500 miles). SRBM are Short Range Ballistic Missiles.

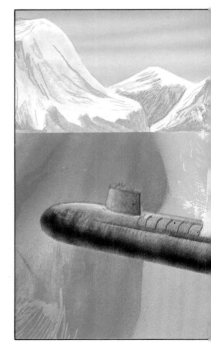

In recent years the trend has been to distinguish weapons by function — a particular necessity, as arms control talks have themselves been broken down into a series of separate discussions. Distinctions here reflect the strategic role of the missiles controlled. Three classes of weapons are particularly important.

Strategic systems (sometimes known as central strategic systems) are weapons designed to be based in the territory of the Superpowers and to be used against the territory of the other Superpower. They also include all ballistic missile submarines not clearly assigned to, and only capable of, attacking targets on the same continent. These are the weapons dealt with under the Strategic Arms Limitation/Reduction talks. They include weapons like US and Soviet ICBMS, submarine based missiles, and long range bombers like the B52.

Theatre nuclear weapons are weapons designed to be used within a theatre of war. As the United States wishes to suggest to the Soviet Union that any nuclear attack on Europe would be met by a US nuclear attack on the Soviet Union, in practice this means weapons that could be used in Europe (including the USSR) in a war in the European theatre. Thus US Pershing II missiles that would retaliate against Soviet targets are part of NATO's Theatre Nuclear Forces. The desire to focus attention on the fact that US missiles from Europe could hit Soviet targets has led to long range weapons in this category being called LRTNF (Long Range Theatre Nuclear Forces). Similarly, the desire to stress the fact that these weapons would often hit the same targets in the USSR as US strategic weapons, has led to weapons that can reach the Soviet Union being known as INF (Intermediate Nuclear Forces). INF are being discussed separately in Geneva. Long Range Theatre Nuclear Forces include US F III strike fighters, Pershing II and Cruise missiles and Soviet Backfire, Blinder and Badger bombers and SS20 and SS4 missiles.

Below the Intermediate nuclear forces exist a number of other nuclear systems, once simply described as tactical nuclear weapons. Today it is possible to differentiate between these by range. Long range systems in this class have ranges less than 1000 km. NATO weapons would be able to hit targets in Eastern Europe but not the Soviet Union, while Soviet weapons fired from Eastern Europe might reach targets in South East England but would not have the range of Soviet systems like the SS20. Such weapons on the Soviet side could perform many of the tasks assigned to Soviet INF in Europe. For NATO they would be of no use as INF replacements, as they could not reach Soviet territory. Even Shorter range weapons have become known as battlefield nuclear weapons. These are designed for use on the battlefield or on Soviet rear echelons moving up to the front. Battlefield weapons would include missiles like the NATO Lance and Soviet SS2l and nuclear artillery shells. Nuclear bombs could be used anywhere on the battlefield or beyond, to the limit of range of the aircraft dropping the bomb.

Finally, nuclear weapons can also be defined by type.

Ballistic missiles are weapons that fly a ballistic trajectory after being thrown into the air by rocket power and, as in ICBM, IRBM, MRBM and SRBM, they are usually subdivided by range. An SLBM is a Submarine Launched Ballistic Missile which in turn is fired from a Ballistic Missile Submarine (SSBN if the submarine is nuclear powered (N) and SSB if powered conventionally).

ABM (Anti-Ballistic Missile) missiles are systems designed to shoot down incoming ballistic missile warheads.

Cruise missiles are weapons that rely on a continuously burning engine to supply their propulsive power. They were deployed as strategic weapons in the 1950s and 1960s and are widely deployed as conventional weapons with ranges up to 500km (300 miles). Recently, with the invention of new engines capable of very long range, they have re-emerged as strategic weapons. These strategic cruise missiles can be divided between GLCM (Ground Launched Cruise Missiles), SLCM (Sea Launched Cruise Missiles) and ALCM (Air Launched Cruise Missiles). Cruise weapons are small, and often fly low to avoid detection. Unlike ballistic missiles, however, they are rather slow and may prove vulnerable to advanced defences designed to shoot them and aircraft down.

Naval nuclear weapons include a variety of nuclear-tipped surface-to-surface (anti-ship) missiles, some nuclear armed air-to-surface missiles and nuclear depth bombs (dropped by helicopters, aircraft and missiles) designed to destroy submerged submarines.

Bombs remain important in both land and sea warfare. They are also among the most difficult weapons to deal with in arms control, as few details are available as to how many exist.

Shells are also important and can weigh as little as 43kg (95 lb). They are even more difficult to count.

A variety of other nuclear devices exist, including mines designed to destroy key communication links in the enemy's path (by producing large impassable craters) and demolition munitions that could be planted by special forces on key targets in the enemy's rear. Although bombers and cruise missiles remain important and may become more so, the majority of today's nuclear weapons are based on ballistic missiles, as shown opposite. The ballistic missile is essentially a rocket with a number of stages to boost it into the trajectory required to hit its target. The rocket motors may be fuelled by a variety of liquid or

Right: The ICBM has taken the science of missile design to extreme refinement. Most of the system is a "brute force" propulsion package designed to elevate the payload into a long-range ballistic trajectory controlled by an onboard computer integrating data from an inertial guidance platform and, quite frequently, a very sensitive star tracker.

Below: Medium-range, intermediate-range and intercontinental ballistic missiles are all capable of strategic roles, and differ most significantly from each other in terms of range. However, the IRBM and ICBM are generally fitted with more advanced penetration aids (penaids) and multiple warheads.

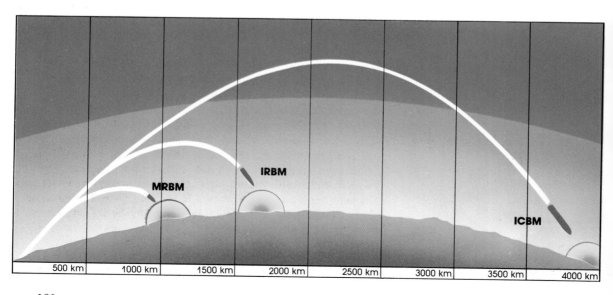

| 500 km | 1000 km | 1500 km | 2000 km | 2500 km | 3000 km | 3500 km | 4000 km |

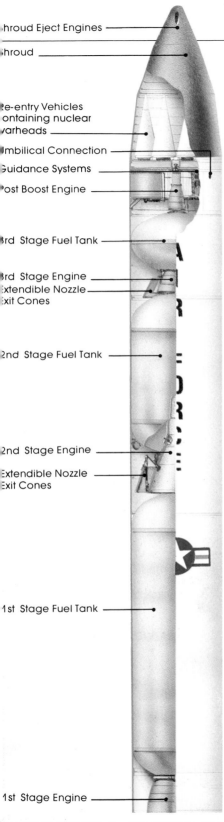

Shroud Eject Engines

Shroud

Re-entry Vehicles
containing nuclear
warheads

Umbilical Connection

Guidance Systems

Post Boost Engine

3rd Stage Fuel Tank

3rd Stage Engine
Extendible Nozzle
Exit Cones

2nd Stage Fuel Tank

2nd Stage Engine

Extendible Nozzle
Exit Cones

1st Stage Fuel Tank

1st Stage Engine

solid chemicals, today storable fuels are the norm. The early missiles relied upon warning time, because they had to be filled with volatile chemicals just before they were fired with some taking days to fill, this was impracticable when an opposing missile could arrive in 30 minutes. Today's missiles, using solid and storable liquid fuels, can be launched in the time taken to react and pull back the concrete and steel slabs that cover the silo: launch times of 1-2 minutes are now normal. Early missiles also stood above ground on gantries, where they were vulnerable to attack. Most land-based missiles are now based in silos — hardened, reinforced, concrete capsules in the ground — where they are safe from all but the nearest nuclear explosions. Recent research on silo construction and the nature of nuclear explosions has suggested that silos could be built with 10 times the hardness of existing ones (silo hardness is measured in terms of PSI [pounds per square inch] of nuclear blast over pressure required to destroy the silo and existing Soviet and US silos are rated at 2000-5000 PSI). This means that a silo should survive unless it is actually in the crater produced by the nuclear explosion.

Once the order to fire is received, has been confirmed and the codes to launch, aim the missile and arm the warhead have been passed on, the missile leaps from its silo into the air. It climbs under the power of its various rocket stages until it reaches the point at which all of its engines have finished firing and dropped away, leaving just the warheads or, in the case of a MIRVed missile (one with Multiple Independently Retargetable Vehicles), a "bus" carrying the nuclear warheads on towards their targets. This initial period is called the boost phase and takes up to five minutes. Some modern missiles have been designed to complete this phase of their flight in under two minutes, allowing them to escape attack. Following the boost phase comes a post-boost phase when, in the case of a MIRVed missile, the post-boost vehicle dispenses its warheads and decoys manoevering in flight to align each warhead with its target. This phase may take up to six minutes. Next comes a mid-course phase lasting 15-20 minutes when the warheads carry on towards their targets, accompanied by a number of penetration aids such as decoys and chaff which fly along the same trajectory to confuse defensive sensors. Finally comes the terminal phase, a period of one to two minutes, when the warheads re-enter the atmosphere. Decoys and chaff may burn up as they re-enter, leaving just the incandescent streak of the warheads in their re-entry vehicles as they fall towards their targets. By this stage an ICBM warhead will have taken perhaps 30 minutes to fly 11,300km (7000 miles) and may have reached an altitude of 1130-1600km (700-1000 miles) on its journey.

Some phases of this flight are particularly crucial. The boost and early post-boost phases are especially important to anyone contemplating defence against ballistic missile attack, because if the enemy missile can be destroyed here, all of its warheads will be destroyed with it. Later, each warhead must be destroyed independently. Missiles are also easier to detect in the boost phase: their engine plumes are readily detectable as they propel the missile upward. The terminal phase also offers some assistance to the defence as the warheads emerge from their cloud of penetration aids. At the moment defensive radars can estimate where

Left: The terrain-comparison (Tercom) guidance of US cruise missiles is designed to update the inertial navigation system. At predetermined times during the flight, the Tercom is turned on to gain a digitally processed image of a presurveyed major landmark, and this is compared with a stored image so that the onboard computer can assess the inertial platform's deviation and issue course corrections. The process is repeated several times to keep the deviation from the planned trajectory to a minimum and so give the missile excellent terminal accuracy.

Below: Once the ICBM has left the atmosphere and discarded its nose cone, the MIRV bus is manoeuvred into exactly the optimum trajectory by its guidance and control system. The bus is then aligned with the first target and at the right moment a warhead is released into the atmosphere together with decoy(s) if necessary. The process is repeated until all the warheads have been deployed.

each warhead will be, and where it will land, by projecting its ballistic trajectory. In the future, this may change as MARV (Manoeuvering Re-Entry Vehicles) are introduced. These could evade defences and perhaps manoeuvre towards their targets by altering their trajectory in flight. Greater investment in more sophisticated penetration aids is also likely, as strategic defences become more threatening.

The modern missile would be nothing without its guidance system. Accuracy is actually far more important than yield in determining what damage a missile will do. As a result the Circular Error Probable (CEP) of a missile is one of the most important guides to a missile's capability. (The CEP is the radius of the circle, in which 50% of the warheads fired by a missile will fall — 50% will therefore fall outside this radius — although something like 99% should fall in a circle with four times the CEP as its radius.) With missiles subject to innumerable perturbations in flight from a range of predictable and unpredictable causes, no missile can be very accurate at ranges much beyond 32.2km (20 miles) without its own internal guidance. External sources of guidance are in danger of being jammed, even if contact can be maintained with the missile, so most missiles carry their own guidance system based on an inertial navigation set with its associated gyros and computers to keep the missile on course. Recently, a new range of sensors has become available for final fixing of the target. These include the Digital Scene Matching Area Correlation (DSMAC) system that matches a stored image of the target area with the actual image seen by the missile, and the RADAG system that similarly matches a radar image of the target to the image seen. Such systems are currently deployed on relatively slow missiles, like the Pershing II, or on some cruise missiles to augment the TERCOM system shown opposite. They would allow even greater accuracy than current weapons. Even without these, however, the gain in accuracy over recent years has been striking. The United States has gone from the Titan II of 1963 with its CEP of 1300 metres (4250') through the 1966 Minuteman II with 370 metres (1200') to the Minuteman III with 150-220 metres (500-700') to the MX with a 90-120 metres (300-400') CEP. The Soviet Union has progressed from the SS7 of 1962 with a CEP of 2750 metres (9000') to the 1966 SS9 at 900 metres (3000') to the current SS18 with a 250 metres (800') CEP. A similar story is true of Submarine Launched Ballistic Missiles, where there is the additional problem of determining the launch vehicle position. Further advances seem likely, perhaps using satellite navigation aids and terminal-homing, manoeuvrable, re-entry vehicles.

The development of nuclear weapons continues, with each new development calling forth new problems and solutions. Recent strategic thinking has been heavily influenced by the three developments shown opposite. The development of "Heavy ICBMs" by the Soviets posed a particular problem for the US because these missiles can carry enough warheads to attack the entire US ICBM force, and are accurate enough to destroy it. The SS18, carrying 10 500 kiloton warheads in its mod four variant, posed a particularly serious threat: the 308 SS18s alone could threaten each of the then 1054 US ICBM silos with a two-warhead attack without even using all 308 missiles or the 360 similarly capable (six-warhead) SSl9 missiles that entered service at the same time. This was a capability which the US had not chosen to develop. The US in the 1970s deployed only 550 of the far smaller Minuteman III (with three warheads each) giving a total of only 1650 warheads which were too few in number to launch the two warheads required at each of the 1400 Soviet ICBM silos. Moreover, the discovery that Soviet ICBM silos were far harder, and more difficult to destroy, than US silos merely served to increase this imbalance. This was one factor in deciding that the strategic debate in the late l970s would focus on the vulnerability of US ICBM: US leaders wondered why the Soviets had built such a capability and whether the US should assume they would never use it.

A second recent development has been the idea of cold-launching. By using compressed gas to drive the missile out of its underground silo rather than the exhaust of its own engines, which now only ignite when the missile is above the ground, it is possible to keep the silo itself relatively intact. The missile gains some additional capability to carry pay-load because it does not have to throw itself out of its silo, and the silo can be re-used if necessary. Soviet introduction of this system for the SS18 raised doubts in the United States as to why the Soviets wanted to have such a reload capability. This was one reason why US analysts began to suggest that the Soviet Union was preparing a capability to fight and survive a nuclear war and to retain intact, refilled missile silos at the end of that war. The US MX missile now being introduced in silos has been designed for cold-launching to give a similar capability.

A third development has been the growing importance of Submarine Launched Ballistic Missiles. Once a relatively minor part of the US and Soviet forces in terms of percentage of warheads deployed, these have become more and more significant. With the introduction of larger missiles and MIRVs, the US submarine force now fields twice as many warheads as the ICBM force. In the Soviet Union the percentage is increasing as MIRVed SLBM enter service with 7–10 warheads replacing old single warhead missiles. The introduction of accurate submarine based missiles will enable more reliance to be placed on the SSBN force if required. The Typhoon class submarine with its twin hulls and 20 SSN20 missiles is perhaps the most visible sign of the increasing importance in Soviet eyes of a capable SSBN force. The SSN20 force alone possesses more warheads on four submarines than the entire Soviet submarine based force did in 1970. While the warheads now have lower yields (six to nine 100 kilotons on the SSN20), they are also more accurate with CEPs of 450 metres (1500') or so. The contrast with the first SLBM, the SSN4 fielded in 1958 with a 2+MT warhead and a CEP of 3.22km (two miles), is striking. Although there is little sign of such a

Right: MIRVed SS-18s are capable of destroying several targets with their independent re-entry vehicles, each carrying up to 10 warheads.

Far right: The use of a cold-launch system (with compressed gas rather than exhaust driving the missile out) means that the SS-18 silo can be reused and the missile can carry a slightly heavier payload.

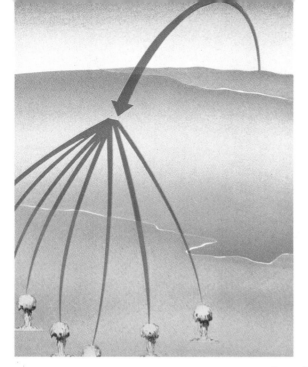

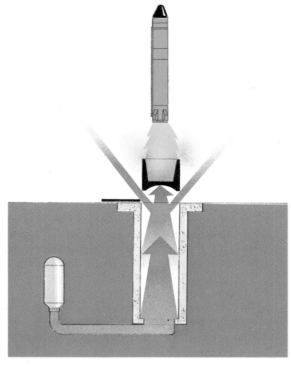

Below: The huge Soviet Typhoon SSBN is at 25,000 tons the World's largest submarine. Designed to operate at sea for long periods with its 20 SSN20 missiles on station to hit targets in the USA.

move, it may be that the attractions of MlRVed, accurate submarine based missiles will grow in the future. If the ability to put large numbers of weapons accurately on target, with a minimum of warning, should prove desirable to either Superpower, this might even lead to a situation where, once again, large numbers of weapons were deployed on submarines just off an opponent's coasts.

US and Soviet Nuclear Forces

As the diagram opposite shows, the years since 1958 have seen the introduction of a large number of different types of nuclear weapon. The number of weapons reflects a variety of factors ranging from the desire to add new capabilities to the force, to maintain a viable force in the light of technical developments in the opponent's defensive or offensive capability, and not least to replace equipment too old to perform reliably in service. Thus short range submarine based missiles have been replaced by longer and longer range missiles, MIRVed missiles have taken over from single warhead missiles, and new bombers have come into service — or more often new weapons for existing bombers have entered the arsenal. Some of the deployments have other motives. The Soviet Union particularly has found it difficult to keep up with Western technology, and seems to have changed or modified its forces more often in a bid to do so. Soviet missile numbers appear to reflect the number of their designers, with new missiles being included in each five or 10 year plan. They may also be less durable than US missiles which seem to last twice as long as their Soviet counterparts.

The diagram below compares today's ICBM ranging from the 218,250kg (485,000lb) weight Soviet SS18 to the 35,055kg (77,900lb) Minuteman III. It can easily be seen that the Soviet Union has consistently deployed more types of ICBM and that these have tended to be larger than their US equivalents. While the United States built relatively few large missiles like the Titan II, the Soviet Union has long placed an emphasis on heavier ICBM. This partly reflects the Soviet aim of getting larger numbers of accurate ICBM warheads and the advantages that come from this, but it may also reflect Soviet design limitations. It is noticeable that the Soviet Union has, for example, had great difficulty in developing solid fuels for missiles and that only the not very successful SS13 was deployed as a solid fuel missile before the

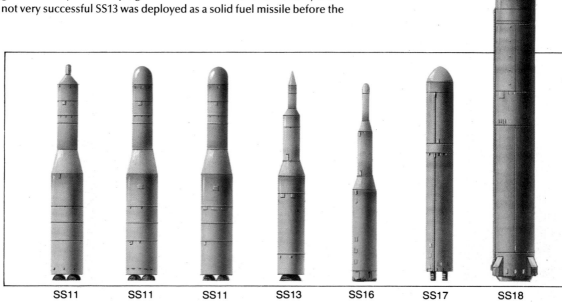

SS11   SS11   SS11   SS13   SS16   SS17   SS18

STRATEGIC NUCLEAR FORCE – MODERNISATION COMPARISON
INTRODUCTION OF SELECTED SYSTEMS BY YEAR

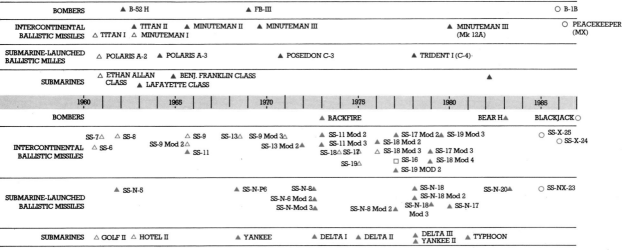

BOMBERS	▲ B-52 H		▲ FB-III			○ B-1B
INTERCONTINENTAL BALLISTIC MISSILES	▲ TITAN II △ TITAN I △ MINUTEMAN I	▲ MINUTEMAN II	▲ MINUTEMAN III		▲ MINUTEMAN III (Mk 12A)	○ PEACEKEEPER (MX)
SUBMARINE-LAUNCHED BALLISTIC MILLES	△ POLARIS A-2 ▲ POLARIS A-3		▲ POSEIDON C-3		▲ TRIDENT I (C-4)·	
SUBMARINES	△ ETHAN ALLAN CLASS ▲ LAFAYETTE CLASS	▲ BENJ. FRANKLIN CLASS			▲	

Timeline: 1960 — 1965 — 1970 — 1975 — 1980 — 1985

BOMBERS				▲ BACKFIRE	BEAR H▲	BLACKJACK○
INTERCONTINENTAL BALLISTIC MISSILES	SS-7△ △ SS-8 △ SS-6	SS-9 Mod 2△ △ SS-9 ▲ SS-11	SS-13△ SS-9 Mod 3△ SS-13 Mod 2▲	▲ SS-11 Mod 2 ▲ SS-11 Mod 3 SS-18△ SS-17▲ SS-19△	▲ SS-17 Mod 2▲ SS-19 Mod 3 ▲ SS-18 Mod 2 △ SS-18 Mod 3 ▲ SS-17 Mod 3 □ SS-16 ▲ SS-18 Mod 4 ▲ SS-19 MOD 2	○ SS-X-25 ○ SS-X-24
SUBMARINE-LAUNCHED BALLISTIC MISSILES	▲ SS-N-5	▲ SS-N-P6	SS-N-8▲ SS-N-6 Mod 2▲ SS-N-Mod 3▲ SS-N-8 Mod 2 ▲	▲ SS-N-18 ▲ SS-N-18 Mod 2 SS-N-18▲ ▲ SS-N-17 Mod 3	SS-N-20▲	○ SS-NX-23
SUBMARINES	△ GOLF II △ HOTEL II		▲ YANKEE	▲ DELTA I ▲ DELTA II	DELTA III ▲ ▲ YANKEE II ▲ TYPHOON	

KEY:
- ▲ ▲ OPERATIONAL SYSTEMS
- △ △ SYSTEMS NOW OUT OF SERVICE
- SS SURFACE TO SURFACE MISSILE
- SS-N SUBMARINE TO SURFACE MISSILE
- ○ ○ SYSTEMS IN FLIGHT TEST

□ SS-16 OPERATIONALLY CAPABLE. AVAILABLE INFORMATION DOES NOT ALLOW CONCLUSIVE JUDGEMENT ON WHETHER THE SOVIET UNION HAS DEPLOYED THE SS-16 BUT DOES INDICATE PROBABLE DEPLOYMENT.

SS24/5 generation of missiles entered service. Soviet superiority in terms of warhead numbers is also not entirely of Soviet making. US leaders made conscious choices to deploy only the small Minuteman missile in the 1960s and 1970s, and they chose only to build a force of 1000-1054 ICBM, versus the Soviet total which reached 1698 in 1975 and which subsequently fell to 1398.

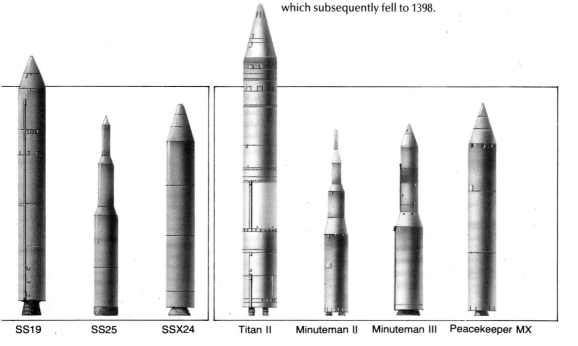

SS19   SS25   SSX24   Titan II   Minuteman II   Minuteman III   Peacekeeper MX

US and Soviet Strategic Force Deployments

The map shows the known sites of Superpower bomber, missile and ballistic missile submarine bases. Such sites are difficult to hide from modern reconnaissance satellites, although there is still no exact way of knowing how many nuclear weapons are deployed at each base. Missile and bomber bases tend to be in the interior of the country, well away from the coasts, in order to give the maximum warning time of attack. This is particularly important for bombers which tend to be based on relatively small numbers of airfields, and which would otherwise be vulnerable to missiles fired from opposing submarines cruising just off the coastline. The United States in particular has moved its bombers more and more to inland sites over the last 10 years. Dispersion of forces may also be useful to ICBM forces as well — with ICBM sites so widely spaced it becomes more difficult to time an attack so that all the warheads arrive on target simultaneously. The need to fire ICBMs at different times to hit different targets at the same time also provides far more information to the opponent's warning sensors. An opponent who has watched warheads fly overhead to more southerly targets, with another wave on his radar screens aimed at northern targets, may be confident enough that he is being attacked to fire his missiles either before or while the first enemy warheads explode. Some new missiles, like the MX, are expressly designed to rise very quickly into the

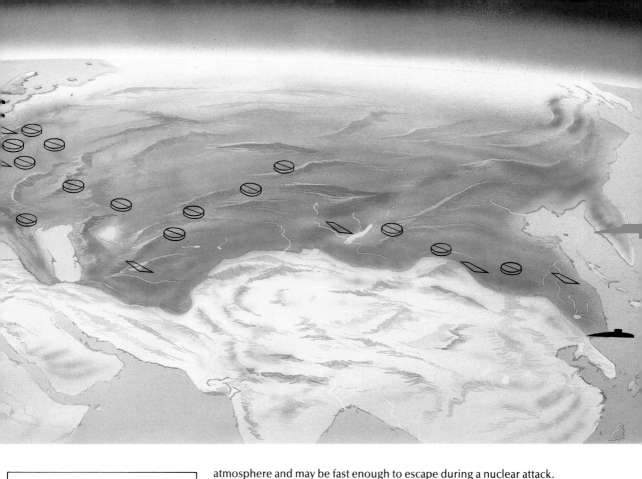

atmosphere and may be fast enough to escape during a nuclear attack. New bombers like the B1 have been designed, and their bases chosen, to ensure that aircraft can also get away from the immediate vicinity of their base quickly enough to avoid any barrage attack around the base. Submarine bases are also carefully sited so that the submarines can easily get into deep water and on patrol, without becoming vulnerable to opposing ASW forces.

The map graphically shows the sheer size of the USA and the Soviet Union, particularly compared to Britain and France. This itself allows far more options than are available in a small country. Soviet ICBMs tend to be spaced out along the enormous length of the Trans-Siberian Railway with the number of sites witnessing the diversity and sheer number of ICBMs. Soviet bombers tend to use forward bases on the Kola Peninsula and other bases in the north, to shorten flight times to America. Soviet submarines have difficulties in the North and would tend to rely on supporting submarines, ships, aircraft and the icecap for protection. In the Far East some would deploy into the Sea of Okhotsk — which the Soviets would attempt to turn into a protected inland sea by deploying defences on and around the Kurile Islands taken from Japan in 1945. The map does not show the increasing importance of the Arctic, Alaska, Iceland, Canada and Greenland, over which most of the missiles and bombers shown would fly to their targets. The trend here is for both sides to improve their warning and defence units facing north, with a view to intercepting bombers or detecting any missile attack.

Minuteman / MX

The MX missile went on alert for the first time in 1986, bringing to an end a long period of discussion about whether and how the United States should deploy a successor to the Minuteman III missile. The MX is the latest in a series of missiles that started with deployment of the Atlas and Titan ICBM in 1958-1960 and then proceeded through the Titan II, Minuteman I and Minuteman II to the Minuteman III. The current force includes 450 of the single warhead Minuteman II's and 550 Minuteman III and MXs. Some four old Titan II missiles, armed with one large 9 MT warhead, remained in service in early 1987, but the intention was to phase these out before the end of the year. Because the MX is a multiple warhead missile and the United States is following SALT limits on numbers of such missiles, introduction of the MX has meant that an equal number of existing MIRV-equipped Minuteman III missiles have been removed from service. MX has thus not replaced the older Minuteman II or Titan missiles which, in Titan's case, have been phased out with no replacement, and in Minuteman II's case will continue in service until some other replacement, like the SICBM, is found.

The problem with MX has been that of finding an acceptable way of basing the missile which would not leave it vulnerable to the scale of first-strike that the Soviet Union's large force of SS18 and SS19 missiles could mount. This anxiety led the Carter Administration both to propose the missile and plan to deploy 200 missiles constantly being shuffled among 4600 shelters. This was designed to cause the Soviets, who would not know which shelters held missiles and who could not destroy more than one shelter with one warhead, to commit 9200 warheads (two per target to allow for failures) to destroy the 200 MX. As this was more warheads than the Soviets were going to deploy on their ICBMs under the terms of SALT II, it was believed that this would remove any Soviet incentive to attack, as it could not succeed. If the Soviets attempted to build more warheads, US planners were certain that they could build concrete shelters far more cheaply than the Soviets could build nuclear warheads and ICBM.

For a variety of reasons the new Reagan Administration in 1981 cancelled this neat, logical but expensive and convoluted plan and since then the MX has looked for a secure base. After exploring a variety of possibilities ranging from siting the missiles so closely that attacking warheads would destroy each other, to burying them hundreds of feet underground, an interim decision was taken to deploy 50 missiles in modified existing Minuteman silos. The first squadron of 10 missiles became operational in this way in 1986. That same year came an announcement that the US Airforce had decided on a safe basing mode for the next 50 missiles. These would be based on 25 trains (two per train) which would leave military areas in crisis to lose themselves on the US rail network. It remains to be seen if Congress approves this idea. Even if it does, the total of MX deployed by the Reagan Administration (100) will still only be half the number required by President Carter in 1979.

Right: Minuteman II.   *Far right: Minuteman III.*

Even when the MX is fully in service, the majority of US ICBM warheads will still be on Minuteman missiles. These will remain in service into the next century with new guidance equipment and motors. It is not clear what will replace these. With all the difficulty of replacing MX, and MX costing $15 billion for just 50 missiles, it seems unlikely that Minuteman will be replaced on a one-for-one basis.

Specification

	BOEING LGM30 G Minuteman III	MARTIN MARIETTA MGM 118 MX
Length	18.3 m (59' 11")	21.64 m (71')
Diameter	168 cm (66")	234 cm (92")
Weight	35,055 kg (77,900 lb)	86,850 kg (193,000 lb)
Range	12,880/14,812 km (8000/9200 miles)	11,270 km (7000+ miles)
Accuracy	150/200 m (500-700') CEP	90 m (300') CEP
Warhead	3 330 kt/170 kt	10 300 kt

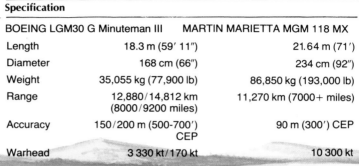

Below: An MX missile newly installed in a former Minuteman III missile silo. The original Minuteman missile is shown at far right in a transporter.

117

SICBM

Anxiety about the survival of fixed site silo-based ICBM and the inability to find and agree a basing mode for the MX ICBM led the US administration to set up the Scowcroft commission to review US requirements and ways of meeting them. The commission suggested that work proceed on a lightweight, land-based, mobile missile which subsequently became known as the Small ICBM or "Midgetman". Funding followed from 1984 with $2.257 billion requested for 1988, following $1.169 billion in 1987.

The SICBM is designed to operate in one of two modes: either constantly moving in time of crisis or operating from a fixed base which it would leave when warning of an attack was received. Current proposals for the carrying vehicle suggest that the complete unit will be able to move across country at 24 km (15 mph) and along roads at over 80 km (50 mph). Thus in the 30 minutes it would take a Soviet ICBM to reach America, the SICBM could move 11.3-40km (7-25 miles). Given that the missile and vehicle are both designed to withstand 7.49 kg/cm^2 (30 PSI) of over pressure from a nearby nuclear explosion (i.e. the SICBM would survive a one megaton bomb going off 2 km (1.3 miles away) this would pose an enormous problem to an attacker who would have to fire 30-370 one megaton warheads to saturate the area where the SICBM could be hiding. If the SICBM were deployed at a large number of sites so that one Soviet barrage would not destroy too many missiles, this would be a very difficult system to counter.

Specification	
	SICBM
Length	14-15.2 metres (47-50')
Diameter	114 cm (45")
Weight	16,650 kg (37,000 lb)
Range	11,109 km (6900 miles)
Accuracy	90 metres (300') CEP
Weight with launcher	96,750 kg (215,000 lbs)
Warhead	1 300 kt warhead plus penetration aids

The SICBM remains the subject of much controversy with critics suggesting a cost of $40-50 billion to deploy 500 missiles with just 500 warheads. Supporters cite the missile's invulnerability. In 1986 proposals to increase the weight of the missile to add one or two more warheads were rejected in favour of retaining mobility by just increasing the weight from 13,500-16,650kg (30-37,000 lb) and adding penetration aids to the warhead. The issues of how many missiles will be built, how many will be based in fixed silos and how many will be mobile remain to be resolved.

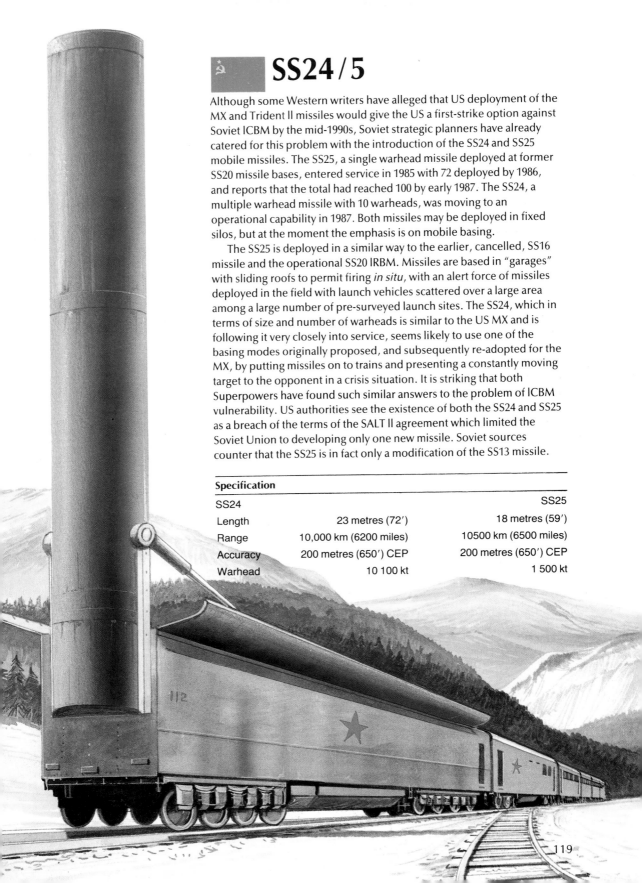

SS24/5

Although some Western writers have alleged that US deployment of the MX and Trident II missiles would give the US a first-strike option against Soviet ICBM by the mid-1990s, Soviet strategic planners have already catered for this problem with the introduction of the SS24 and SS25 mobile missiles. The SS25, a single warhead missile deployed at former SS20 missile bases, entered service in 1985 with 72 deployed by 1986, and reports that the total had reached 100 by early 1987. The SS24, a multiple warhead missile with 10 warheads, was moving to an operational capability in 1987. Both missiles may be deployed in fixed silos, but at the moment the emphasis is on mobile basing.

The SS25 is deployed in a similar way to the earlier, cancelled, SS16 missile and the operational SS20 IRBM. Missiles are based in "garages" with sliding roofs to permit firing *in situ*, with an alert force of missiles deployed in the field with launch vehicles scattered over a large area among a large number of pre-surveyed launch sites. The SS24, which in terms of size and number of warheads is similar to the US MX and is following it very closely into service, seems likely to use one of the basing modes originally proposed, and subsequently re-adopted for the MX, by putting missiles on to trains and presenting a constantly moving target to the opponent in a crisis situation. It is striking that both Superpowers have found such similar answers to the problem of ICBM vulnerability. US authorities see the existence of both the SS24 and SS25 as a breach of the terms of the SALT II agreement which limited the Soviet Union to developing only one new missile. Soviet sources counter that the SS25 is in fact only a modification of the SS13 missile.

Specification		
SS24		SS25
Length	23 metres (72')	18 metres (59')
Range	10,000 km (6200 miles)	10500 km (6500 miles)
Accuracy	200 metres (650') CEP	200 metres (650') CEP
Warhead	10 100 kt	1 500 kt

SLBM

Ballistic missile submarines have featured in Superpower nuclear arsenals since 1958. Today, approximately 125 are in service with the US, Chinese, British and French forces. The Soviet Union fields a force of 62 modern and 13 older conventionally powered boats with the US fielding 28 Lafayette, Madison and Franklin and eight Trident class. Both fleets show how the submarine-based element of the nuclear force has evolved in the last 20 years. The Soviets still field their original, conventionally powered ballistic missile submarine, the Golf class, as part of their theatre nuclear forces in the Far East and Europe. In their strategic force they still retain some Yankee class nuclear powered ballistic missile submarines built in the 1960s but are taking these out of service, and converting some to carry nuclear-tipped cruise missiles, to stay within the limits defined by the SALT agreements. The main component of the force is the Delta Class which have been progressively enlarged to take larger missiles. The biggest submarines in the world (and in history) are the new Typhoon class which are being produced at the rate of one a year. These are monsters at 25,000 tons and are designed to be quiet and give long endurance. The US has passed through a similar transition with the 10 old Ethan Allen and George Washington classes phased out for similar reasons to the Yankee class, the Lafayette class being updated to the Poseidon missile (16 boats) and the Trident I missile (12 boats) with the new Ohio class, designed to spend more of its life at sea and to be quieter than any other submarine, weighing in at 18,700 tons.

The Submarine Launched Ballistic Missile plays an increasingly important role in nuclear strategy for a variety of reasons. The failure of any power to find a means of finding submerged Ballistic Missile Submarines (SSBN) on patrol has meant that the submarine based part of the nuclear deterrent has become increasingly important as the land-based bombers and ICBM have become more and more vulnerable. The invention of new means of locating the exact position of the submarine prior to launch, and new methods of guiding the missile in flight, combined with the availability of new missiles able to carry multiple warheads, now allows the SLBM to perform many of the missions formerly performed by land-based ICBM. The SSBN has also been seized upon by the second rank of nuclear powers as their preferred deterrent weapon with Britain operating four boats, France six and China putting SLBM to sea on two classes of nuclear-powered submarines. With some commentators seeing an increasing function for British and French nuclear forces providing a nuclear deterrent in Europe, and China placing a high priority on its forces, these forces seem likely to assume even greater importance in the future.

At present Ballistic Missile Submarines retain their relatively high degree of invulnerability when deployed at sea. The trends are for submarines to become quieter and quieter which makes their detection by sonar more and more difficult. The increase in range of Submarine Launched Ballistic Missiles has also made the problem of tracking submarines more difficult, as they have far more water to hide in. The early Submarine Launched Ballistic Missiles had exceedingly short

The picture right shows some of the forces that would be involved in a modern ASW campaign. ASW is now a three-dimensional problem involving satellites, ships, shore bases, aircraft, helicopters and submarines.

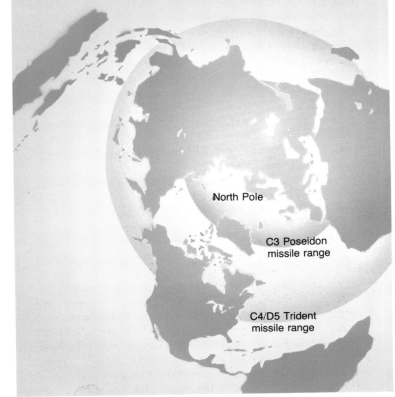

The map right shows how the greater range of modern missiles allows US ballistic missile submarines to keep their missiles within range of their targets from larger and larger areas of ocean. With such areas to hide in, ASW against the submarines becomes a practically impossible task.

North Pole

C3 Poseidon
missile range

C4/D5 Trident
missile range

ranges, in the case of the Soviet SSN4 this, effectively meant that they had to be deployed in the eastern Mediterranean and off the US coastline. Today the Soviet SSN 18, 20 and 23 have ranges of 6500 km, 8300 km and 8300 km (4040, 5160 and 5160 miles) respectively, while the US Trident C4 has a range of 6400 km (4000 miles). This allows the Soviet ballistic missile submarine force to keep its missiles within reach of US targets while they are deployed in the Greenland and Barents seas and the Sea of Okhotsk in the Far East. They could even fire their missiles from alongside in their shore bases if necessary. The Soviet Union anyway seems less concerned about the prospect of surprise attack as it keeps a far lower proportion of its submarines at sea than the US which keeps 50%-70% of its force on daily patrol. This may, however, reflect practical problems as much as choice on the Soviets' behalf. The extended range available with the Trident missiles has meant that US submarines (and later the British) can now patrol wide areas of the Pacific and Atlantic and can hide in 43×10^6 km^2 (16.5 million square miles) of ocean compared to the 6.5×10^6 km^2 (2.5 million square miles) available beforehand. With submarines on patrol operating on the principle of avoiding any contact with any other ships, with the depths of the ocean to hide in, and with the submarine moving at slow speed to avoid making noise, the task of finding a submarine in this volume of water remains rather like the hunt for the needle in the haystack.

This does not mean, however, that there are not active efforts underway to hunt for opposing SSBN. Experiments are continually made to evaluate other sensors that do not rely on sound to detect the submarines — as yet all of these have proved either only to work at very short ranges or to be ineffective against submarines at normal operating depths. More traditional means are also tried with the Soviet Navy having put a particularly strong effort into hunting SSBN with its own hunter-killer submarines. It is generally assumed that SSBN bases would also be a prime target for Soviet minelaying forces, and US officials have expressed anxiety that US Atlantic bases could be mined by Cuban submarines. Soviet leadership is also concerned about its own SSBN force. Concern that all the Soviet submarines in the Atlantic were found by US forces in the Cuban Missile crisis of 1962 was one factor that led the Soviet Union to deploy most of its SSBN near its own coastline. A feeling that the West could still find these submarines has led to the Soviets deploying them in defended areas (bastions) where they are protected against Western ships, aircraft and submarines. This is no small undertaking, particularly as the Soviets see their submarines as part of their strategic reserve which would have to be kept operational for a long period in a nuclear or conventional war.

The map illustrates operations that might be conducted by Soviet naval forces. Most Soviet units would probably be retained in the Barents and Greenland Seas to protect Soviet SSBN. Some units would form a defensive barrier in the Norwegian Sea to stop NATO forces moving North. Some submarines and aircraft would attempt to attack shipping in the Atlantic whilst Black Sea and Mediterranean based units attacked the US Sixth Fleet. Finally forward deployed SSBN would attempt to survive and keep their missiles targeted on the USA.

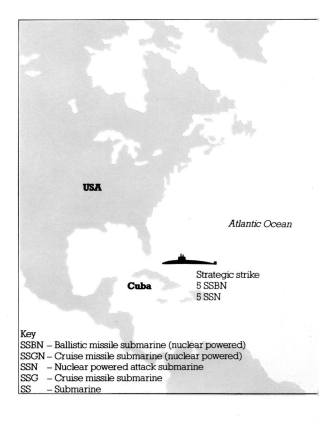

USA

Atlantic Ocean

Strategic strike
5 SSBN
5 SSN

Cuba

Key
SSBN – Ballistic missile submarine (nuclear powered)
SSGN – Cruise missile submarine (nuclear powered)
SSN – Nuclear powered attack submarine
SSG – Cruise missile submarine
SS   – Submarine

Indeed, it is estimated that in wartime the bulk of the Soviet Navy would be engaged in defending these nuclear forces.

Although they have been trying to do the same to Western SSBN for many years, the Soviets have some cause for anxiety. US leaders have recently acknowledged that, in wartime, their submarines would try to destroy Soviet SSBN. US thinking about how to fight and win a maritime war stresses the importance of fighting an offensive campaign rather than sitting back and allowing the Soviet Union to dominate Norway and Japan. This would see a massive air and sea engagement, particularly in the Norwegian sea. If the US Navy won this, it would be free to attack Soviet SSBN, their bases and the Soviet land-mass itself, at its leisure. Some US writers have even suggested that the prospect of losing their SSBN, or saving them by starting a nuclear war at sea to stop the US Navy, may itself be enough to deter any Soviet leader from starting any war in Europe.

Changes are also occurring in how submarine forces are deployed and operated. Partly to escape the attentions of Western ASW forces, Soviet submarines are now reported to be using the Arctic ice to hide themselves. In a sign of the increasing complexity of the submarine world, US submarines are now being fitted out to, and the follow-on class of submarine is being designed to, operate under the ice.

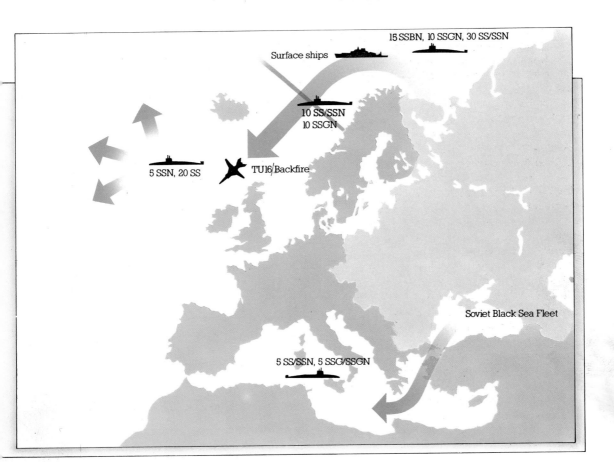

15 SSBN, 10 SSGN, 30 SS/SSN

Surface ships

10 SS/SSN
10 SSGN

5 SSN, 20 SS   TU16/Backfire

Soviet Black Sea Fleet

5 SS/SSN, 5 SSG/SSGN

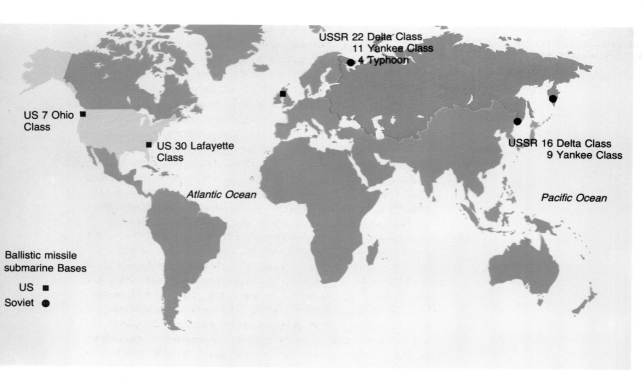

USSR 22 Delta Class
11 Yankee Class
4 Typhoon

US 7 Ohio
Class

US 30 Lafayette
Class

USSR 16 Delta Class
9 Yankee Class

Atlantic Ocean

Pacific Ocean

Ballistic missile
submarine Bases

US ■
Soviet ●

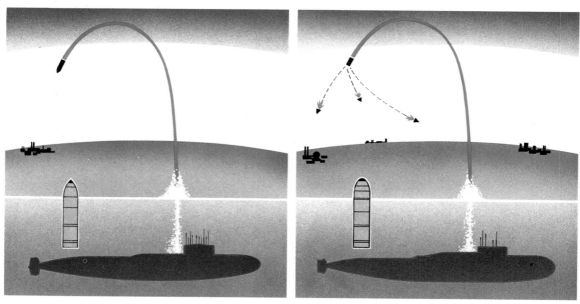

Left: SS-NX-17 fired from Yankee II.
  Submarine carries only single re-entry
  vehicle.

Right: SS-N-18 fired from a Delta III.
  Submarine carries 3 MIRVs.

eft: US and Soviet ballistic missile
ubmarine bases and the deployment of
SBNs in the Atlantic and Pacific Oceans.

Presumably they will be hunting the same Soviet SSBN. Since 1983 Soviet Delta class submarines have also been operating off the US coastline, even though they could hit the US from long-range (unlike the Yankee class which still have the short-ranged, 3000 km (1860 mile) SSN6 missile). Such submarines were deployed to threaten a response on US targets if the US used the new LRTNF missiles it was emplacing in Europe. They may also offer Soviet leaders new options. With missiles with multiple warheads off the US coastline, a Soviet surprise attack could be far more devastating than it could in the age of single warheads.

At present no replacement for the SSBN is in sight. Both the Soviet Navy and the US Navy are deploying large numbers of nuclear-tipped, strategic land-attack cruise missiles. However, these seem to be a complement to rather than a replacement for the ballistic missile. No nuclear power has chosen to rely on the cruise missile as its sole deterrent and both Great Britain and France have concluded that cruise would not offer them a viable deterrent. Cruise is slow, relatively vulnerable to modern air defences, and relatively short-ranged, with the result that large numbers would have to be deployed in a relatively small area of water to achieve the same effect as a far smaller ballistic missile force. Unless deployment of strategic defences makes ballistic missiles more vulnerable, it seems unlikely that cruise missiles will replace ballistic ones. Cruise missiles would bring other problems, too, as the small size of cruise missiles means that they pose more of a problem for arms control which rests on the ability to count the numbers of missiles on each side. A greater threat may come from the development of mobile land-based missiles which can use mobility to mimic the SSBN's vulnerability. In the long term it remains to be seen whether mobile land-based missiles can provide the same degree of invulnerability or be as cost-effective as the ballistic missile hiding at sea on a missile submarine.

There may be a problem in dealing with the difficulties of increasing costs and arms control agreements which drastically reduce nuclear forces. The trend towards large submarines and multiple warheads is also a trend to smaller numbers of submarines. The Soviet Union is currently maintaining a level of 62 ballistic missile submarines but may follow the US example and reduce this as weapons become more expensive. The US force, which totalled 41 submarines from the 1960s to the late 1970s, is now reducing to a force level of only 20 Ohio class submarines. Although better reactors, more reliable missiles and larger submarines allow more time at sea, this will inevitably lead to a situation where perhaps only 13 submarines were at sea compared with the 22 or so available in the early 1970s. This problem of so many eggs in so few baskets would be worsened by agreement to major reductions in strategic force levels. It would put even more of a premium on strategic anti-submarine warfare and might actually make the strategic balance less stable.

Trident II

Trident II (D5) is the US Navy's sixth SLBM following the Polaris AI, A2 and A3, Poseidon C3 and Trident I (C4). It is the largest missile with a range of 9660km (6000 miles) and the ability to carry up to I4 warheads. In US service some of this range will be traded off for payload and no more than 8-10 warheads may be deployed. The warheads, however, will be heavy enough and accurate enough to pose a retaliatory threat to all types of target, including hardened missile silos and command posts. However, this does not mean that the Trident II will have the first strike potential alleged by critics. Although the missile has a variety of sensors that make it more accurate than most land-based missiles, its warhead is still not large enough to pose a threat to Soviet ability to command and control their nuclear forces by destroying their command posts. Nor is there yet any solution to the problem of how to communicate instantly and reliably with a submerged submarine force spread throughout the world's oceans. Without this capability, a first strike could at best not be co-ordinated, and at worst would fail as various submarines failed to get their instructions. US naval sources suggest that the SLBM fleet will remain a retaliatory force which will either stay in reserve to deter against major nuclear attacks, or which could at best only be used several hours into a nuclear war as surviving US command and control systems issued orders to their submarines telling them what retaliatory action was required.

Trident II is to become operational in I989 when it will be deployed on the ninth Ohio class ballistic missile submarine. It is thought that eventually the force will total 20-23 boats with the first eight being backfitted from their current C4 missiles to the D5. Partly because of the size of the missile and partly to give greater protection, the Ohio class submarines are the largest built by any Western navy at 18,700 tons.

In I983 the United Kingdom decided to purchase the Trident D5 to provide the next generation of the British deterrent. The first British 15,000 ton submarine, HMS Vanguard, may enter service in 1994. Given that the missile may have a 30-year life, and that its size allows room for future modification, Trident missiles may still be providing part of the Western nuclear deterrent in the late 2020s.

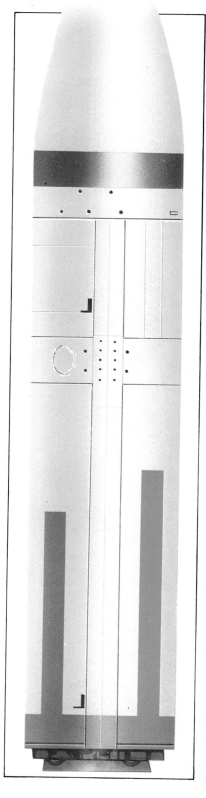

Specification

	Polaris A3	Poseidon	Trident II
Length	9.7 metres (32′)	10.3 metres (34′)	13.4 metres (44′ 6″)
Diameter	138cm (54″)	187cm (74″)	210cm (83″)
Weight	16,065 kg (35,700 lb)	29,250 kg (65,000 lb)	58,500 kg (130,000 lb)
Range	4636.8 km (2880 miles)	4000/5200 km (2485/3230 miles)	6400/9660 km (4000/6000 miles)
Accuracy	800 metres (2600′) CEP	550 metres (1800′) CEP	120 metres (400′) CEP
Warhead	3 200 kt	10-14 40 kt	8-14 475 kt

# M4

Since the first French ballistic missile submarine, the Redoubtable, entered service in l971 with the M1 missile, France has deployed three types of Submarine Launched Ballistic Missiles. Following the M1 with a range of 2175 km (1350 miles) and a single 500kt warhead came the M2 with the same warhead and a range of 3000 km (1875 miles) the M20 with a range of 3000 km (1875 miles) and a 1.2 megaton warhead and the M4 with six 150 kt warheads and 4500 + km (2800 + mile) range. The M4 is France's first multiple warhead missile, with some sources claiming that each warhead has a capability to attack an independent target, and others arguing that the system is a MRV where all six warheads fall in a shot-gun pattern towards one main target area. The M4 is a large missile and although the US missile carries more warheads further and has a true MIRV capability, it is comparable in some ways to the US Trident I (C4) missile.

France is determined to maintain the capability of her nuclear deterrent into the foreseeable future and if possible to add to the credibility of that deterrent by increasing the number and the scale of the options available to the French President. To do this, and to maintain a capability of penetrating any defence systems that the Superpowers may erect between 1995 and 2020, the French government is proceeding with a number of measures to maintain an effective deterrent. It is planned that the M4 will be replaced by a true MIRV missile, the M5, carrying 9-12 warheads in the 1990s. These missiles would be operated from a new class of 14,000 ton submarines as France follows the logic which has led the British, Soviets and Americans to similarly large submarines and missiles. This force will also acquire much of the infrastructure that is currently only possessed by the Superpowers as the French deploy an airborne command post to ensure communications with the SNLE force, increase the capability of the rest of the fleet to support the force, and deploy new communication and reconnaissance satellites that may have a strategic mission.

Specification

AÉROSPATIALE M4	
Length	11 metres (36′)
Diameter	193 cm (76″)
Weight	34,722 kg (77,160 lb)
Range	4500-6760 km (2800-4200 miles)
Warhead	6 150 kt

Air Launched Cruise Missile (ALCM)

The Air Launched Cruise Missile (ALCM) entered US service in 1981 on the B52G bomber. Strategic cruise missiles are not, however, a new idea. The ALCM in fact is the successor to the Snark, Mace, Matador and Regulus weapons deployed by the US armed forces from 1951-1969 and long range stand-off bombs like the Hound Dog carried by US bombers from 1958-1975. Similar tactical and strategic missiles and stand-off bombs also entered service with British and Soviet forces. The ALCM differs in using advances in fuel, engine, guidance and warhead technology to produce more range and far greater accuracy and reliability in a much smaller missile. This means that while the B52 could only carry two Hound Dogs, it can now carry 12-20 ALCM, which in turn allows enough missiles to be fired to saturate a defence.

The introduction of a terrain comparison guidance system has also brought new options. The cruise missile can fly low as it is expressly designed to follow the contours of the ground. It can also navigate accurately to its target which allows either a smaller warhead to be carried or greater certainty that the target will be destroyed. The provision of an extra targeting system in the form of a Digital Scene Matching system, as fitted on the sea-based conventional-attack cruise missile, would even give enough accuracy to use conventional warheads for some missions if such a capability was desired.

The Boeing AGM 86B ALCM was the winner of a 1978 competition between it and the General Dynamics AGM 109 to provide a cruise missile for use on Strategic Air Command Bombers. This was in the aftermath of President Carter's 1977 decision to rely on cruise missiles instead of the B1A bomber which was promptly cancelled. The AGM 109 went on to become the basis of the Air Force's Ground Launched Cruise Missile (GLCM) and the Navy's Sea Launched Cruise Missile (SLCM). Original plans were to buy up to 4300 ALCM, but production of the AGM 86 ended in 1986 with 1700-1800 built. This was to allow transition to building l300 of an improved Advanced Cruise Missile (ACM) in 1989. The ACM would have more range than the AGM 86 4000 km (2400 miles), greater speed, and would incorporate a variety of stealth techniques to make it less vulnerable. SAC also intends to field a new Short Range Attack Missile (SRAM II) which would mean that Soviet defences would have to deal with 3000 cruise missiles, plus SRAM and bomb-armed bombers, all trying to penetrate its defences at the same time. Moreover, the cruise missiles and bombers would only arrive at their targets six to eight hours into a nuclear war, by which stage defences would be far weaker. It is not clear that a few cruise missiles going against Soviet air defences on their own would survive against the weight of missiles, fighters and airborne warning aircraft that would be used against them. In numbers, and used with other forces, however, cruise missiles offer a strong deterrent to anyone hoping to fight and win nuclear war.

Cruise is now deployed on over 135 B52G and H bombers and the US has continued to deploy bombers even though only 132 are allowed by the SALT II agreement. Since 1984 the Soviet Union has deployed its own ALCM, the AS15, and is developing a supersonic cruise missile that may be deployed on aircraft as well as submarines.

Specification	
BOEING AGM 86B ALCM	
Length	6.5 metres (20' 9")
Diameter	64 cm (25")
Weight	1271.25 kg (2825 lb)
Range	2780 km (1725 miles)
Accuracy	75 metres (250')

inertial naviga

flight control ele

bulk memory element

radar altimeter
electronics

air data

radar altimeter
antennae

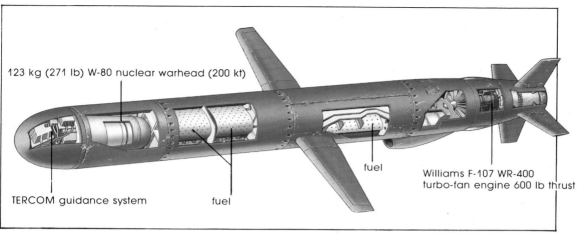

123 kg (271 lb) W-80 nuclear warhead (200 kt)

TERCOM guidance system

fuel

fuel

Williams F-107 WR-400
turbo-fan engine 600 lb thrust

Below: The key to the cruise missile is a simplicity of concept with extreme sophistication of detail design in areas such as the avionics (flight-control and guidance systems), airframe (flight surfaces folded into the main length of the missile for deployment only after the weapon has been launched), powerplant (miniaturised and *designed to last for only a few hours to reduce cost and weight), and the compact but effective warhead. The AGM-86 epitomises all these features, which allow many such missiles to be carried by existing platforms (Boeing B-52 Stratofortress and the Rockwell B-1B).* *Above: Tomahawk SLCM/GLCM cruise missile – nuclear land attack version.*

turbofan engine (Williams Research Corp. F-107 WR-100 turbofan developing 600 lb thrust)

heat exchanger

rate gyro

payload envelope (W.80 nuclear warhead)

wing deploy actuators

US Bombers

Bombers have traditionally played a major role in the US nuclear deterrent. In the 1950s the US deployed the B36 long range and B47 medium range bombers, and followed these with the introduction of 744 B52s from 1955 onwards. The B52 A-F have since been phased out, but 98 B52H and 165 B52G remain in service with the Strategic Air Command (SAC) supported by 61 FB IIIA medium bomber versions of the F III strike fighter. Unlike the Royal Air Force where the last of the V Bombers, the Vulcan, was replaced by the Tornado GRI fighter in 1983, and France, where it is envisaged that the last 34 Mirage IV bombers will be replaced in the mid-1990s by shorter range Mirage 2000N strike fighters, the US Air Force does see a continuing need for long range aircraft. To this end, it is currently introducing the B1 B bomber and intends to follow this with the "stealth" bomber, the B2, in 1992.

The B52 remains the principal US strategic bomber even though the aircraft first flew in 1952. Although the B52G and H versions still in service were all built between 1959 and 1962, this still means that the aircraft are now at least 25 years old — which produces the situation where the pilots are sometimes younger than their aircraft. Despite this, the aircraft is still thought to be effective. Since the 1970s the basic aircraft has been refitted with a variety of new electronic countermeasures equipment, night vision cameras, navigation equipment and new communications which should keep it viable in the all-weather low-level penetration role. Ninety-eight B52Gs are also being fitted as launchers for 12 Air Launched Cruise Missiles (ALCM) and conversion of 96 B52 H to do the same continues. Under current plans, the B52G (ALCM) will probably continue in service to 1992 at least, and the B52Hs will serve as dual role cruise missile carriers and penetrators (i.e. they will fire their cruise missiles and then carry on to penetrate Soviet air defences using short-range missiles and bombs) until 1992, when they will revert to being just ALCM carriers. It is not clear when the B52H or 61 B52G which already have a conventional bombing role will be replaced. It is likely that the B52H will still be in service in 2000.

Since 1986 the B52 has been joined by the B1 B with the force rapidly building up to reach 100 aircraft by 1988. The B1 B is the successor to the B1 A version of the aircraft cancelled by President Carter in 1978 in favour of relying on the old B52s with ALCM. The B1 B is currently having some teething problems and will not reach its full capability until 1988. It does, however, still promise to be a great advance on the B52 with far more advanced electronic countermeasures, greater weapons carriage capability, greater speed at low level and a far smaller radar image to attract attention. When the B2 comes into service, the B1 B may be fitted with cruise missiles to give it a stand-off role. The next US strategic bomber will be the B2 or stealth bomber. This is expected to fly in 1987 with an in-service date in the early 1990s. The stealth bomber is designed to use a variety of means to reduce its radar, sound and visual image so that it can only be detected at very short range, if at all. On current thinking 132 B2s would be built, taking over responsibility for penetrating Soviet air defence from the B52H and the B1 B. The final size of the bomber force, just how many B2s will be built and how many B52s

Specification

B52H

Weight	227,250 kg (505,000 lb)
Range	12,000 to 16,250 km (7500-10,100 miles)
Penetration speed	555-650 km (345-405 mph)
Maximum speed	960 kmph (595 mph)
Warload	22,500 kg (45,000 lb)

B1 B

Weight	214,650 kg (477,000 lb)
Range	12000 km (7500 miles)
Penetration speed	980 kmph (610 mph)
Maximum speed	Mach 1.25
Warload	56,250 kgm (125,000 lb)

B2

Weight	180,000 kg (400,000 lb)
Range	9260 km (5750 miles)
Penetration speed	N/A
Maximum speed	980 kmph (608 mph)
Warload	18,000 kg (40,000 lb)

Rockwell International B-1B

Boeing B-52, Stratofortress

retained, is not yet clear, and will depend on the outcome of current arms control talks. As well as new bombers the late 1980s and early 1990s will see a considerable array of new weapons as the current B28, B43, B61 and B83 bombs and AGM 69 Short Range Attack (SRAM) and AGM 86 cruise missiles are joined by the new SRAM 2 missile and the Advanced Cruise Missile.

Some other developments are notable. The first is that SAC is placing more and more emphasis on conventional operations. It currently plans to have 235 B52s and 90 B1 Bs available for conventional missions. 61 B52s are already used for maritime reconnaissance and strike using Harpoon anti-ship missiles and minelaying as well as conventional heavy bombing. They are assigned to the US rapid deployment force and would be used early in any conflict involving that force. When and if stand-off weapons like the 24 km (15 mile) range AGM 130 bomb and its possible successors, including perhaps a conventionally armed cruise missile, enter service, the potential will exist to launch world-wide, conventional, precision attacks from the United States itself.

Such attacks would rely extensively on SAC's often forgotten but vital tanker force which is also being reworked. It currently comprises 615 operational KC135 tankers which are operated by a variety of SAC, Reserve and Air National Guard squadrons. Although 60 new KC 10 tanker versions of the DC 10 airliner are being procured, the KC 135 (itself a relative of the earlier Boeing 707 airliner) is destined to provide Strategic tanker support into the next century. Although some aircraft are being given new technology engines and other improvements, it may be 2020 before a successor is found. By then the KC135 will have stood alert as part of US strategic forces for 63 years.

Soviet Bombers

Although the Soviet Union has placed most priority since 1957 on its missile forces, bombers remain an important part of the Soviet nuclear arsenal. In the 1950s the Soviets built 1200 + copies of the American B29 as the Tupolev Tu 4. This was followed by a series of medium and heavy bombers that are soon to be joined by the new Blackjack strategic bombers. Indeed, with the Blackjack being introduced and cruise missiles coming into service, the Soviet Long Range Air Force seems to be having something of a renaissance. Moves to develop defences against ballistic missiles could only serve to speed up this revival.

The Soviet medium bomber force, all nuclear capable, totals 510 aircraft and is made up of 240 Tu 16 Badger, 130 Tu 22 Blinder and 140 Tu 22M Backfire bombers. In addition, the Soviet Naval Air Arm has 395 aircraft of the same types that could be committed to attacks on land targets. The newest of these is the Backfire which came into service in 1977 and may be able to reach US targets on a one-way mission or if refuelled in flight.

The current main heavy bomber is the Tu 20 Bear which entered service in 1956 and is still being built. The 140 Bears are supported by 20 or so surviving Mya 4 bombers which may have been converted to a refuelling role. The Bear force is currently expanding as new Bear H aircraft capable of carrying four to twelve AS 15 cruise missiles enter service. The force is also becoming more capable as new AS 4 missiles enter service on older Tu 20s. The last two years have seen an increase in Soviet activity off the US and Canadian borders, as Tu 20Hs practise flying to their cruise missile release points. As a result there is an upgrading programme under way for both US and Canadian Air defences.

Specification

TU 16
Weight	71,100 kg (158,000 lb)
Range	5750 km (3580 miles)
Speed	990 kmph (616 mph)
Warload	9000 kg (20,000 lb)

TU 22
Weight	84,000 kg (185,000 lb)
Range	6200 km (3875 miles)
Speed	Mach 1.4
Warload	540 kg (12,000 lb)

TU 22M
Weight	121,500 kg (270,000 lb)
Range	8900 km (5530 miles)
Speed	Mach 2
Warload	9900 kg (22,000 lb)

TU 20
Weight	153,000 kg (340,000 lb)
Range	12.500 km (7800 miles)
Speed	870 kmph (540 mph)
Warload	11,250 kg (25,000 lb)

Blackjack
Weight	261,000 kg (380,000 lb)
Range	14,600 km (9075 miles)
Speed	Mach 2.3
Warload	N/A

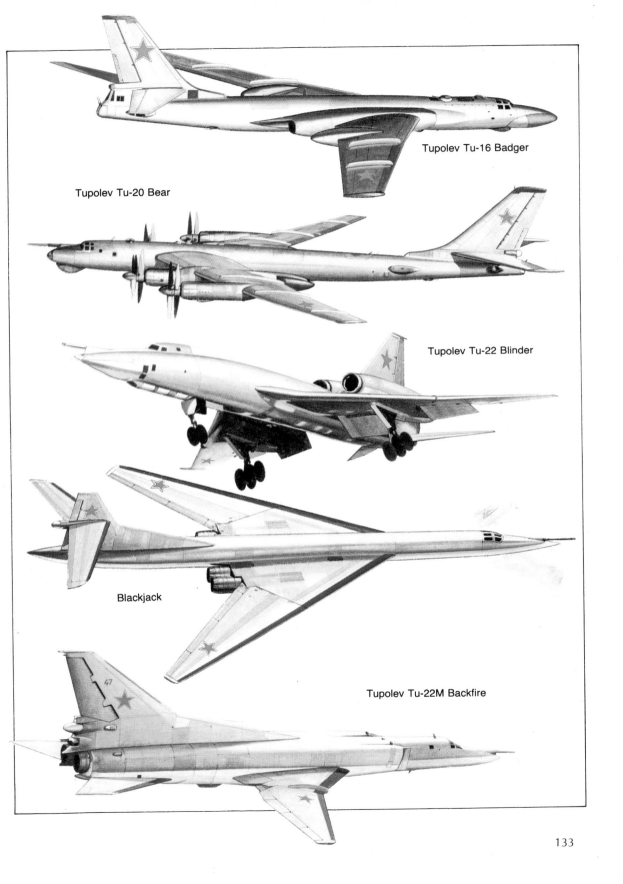

Tupolev Tu-16 Badger

Tupolev Tu-20 Bear

Tupolev Tu-22 Blinder

Blackjack

Tupolev Tu-22M Backfire

Pershing II

Since 1983, 108 of the single warhead Pershing II missiles have been deployed by the US Army in West Germany. This was part of the response agreed by NATO in 1979 to the growing imbalance in theatre nuclear weapons created by Soviet deployment of new systems, including the Backfire bomber and SS20 missile. The Pershing IIs replace an identical number of Pershing I missiles that were first deployed in 1962. The Pershing II, however, has far more range than the Pershing I 1810 v 740 km (1125 miles v 460) which permits it to meet the requirement to be able to hit targets in the western Soviet Union. This allows the Pershing II to threaten to hit Soviet targets if Soviet weapons were exploded on NATO territory, and was intended to remove any belief the Soviets might have that a nuclear war could be fought in Europe with no damage to the Soviet Union. Pershing II is also far more accurate with its Radar Area-correlation Guidance System (RADAG) which matches a stored radar image of the missile's target, with the radar image seen by the missile to make final corrections as it falls towards its target. Pershing II also has a lower yield warhead than Pershing I. This combination of accuracy and yield increases the options available for its use and would drastically reduce the area of damage caused by the warhead. Pershing II would only take 12-14 minutes to reach a target in the Soviet Union, but the weapon's range and the low numbers deployed mean that it poses little threat to Soviet nuclear forces. Though it was proposed to deploy an earth-penetrating warhead to attack underground command posts, it is believed that this was not proceeded with. Like Pershing I, Pershing II is fired from a mobile vehicle which would operate from hidden, pre-selected and surveyed sites in time of crisis. The earlier Pershing I continues in service with the West German Air Force which operates 72 launchers with US nuclear warheads under a dual-key arrangement.

Top right: The key to the Pershing 2's accuracy lies in the Goodyear-manufactured RADAG (Radar Area Guidance) system. This becomes operational in the terminal phase of the flight, and compares active radar returns from the target area with stored images of the area; computer correlation of the two then generates steering commands for the re-entry vehicle, resulting in so great a degree of accuracy that only a modest nuclear warhead need be fitted.

Specification

MARTIN MARIETTA MGM 31 PERSHING 1

Length	10.5 metres (34' 6")
Diameter	100 cm (40")
Weight	4570 kg (10,150 lb)
Range	740 km (460 miles)
Accuracy	400 metres (1300') CEP
Guidance	Inertial
Warhead	1 60-400 kt

PERSHING II

Length	10.5 metres (34' 6")
Diameter	100 cm (40")
Weight	7380 kg (c 16,400 lb)
Range	1810 km (1125 miles)
Accuracy	37 metres (120') CEP
Guidance	Inertial + RADAG
Warhead	1 5-500 kt

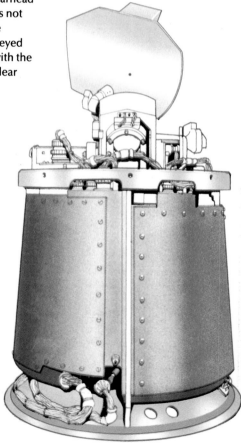

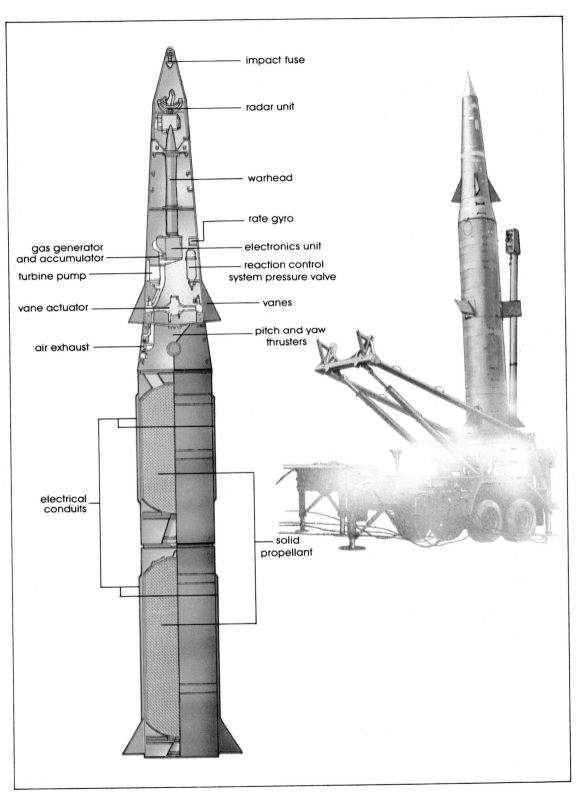

impact fuse

radar unit

warhead

rate gyro

gas generator
and accumulator

electronics unit

turbine pump

reaction control
system pressure valve

vane actuator

vanes

pitch and yaw
thrusters

air exhaust

electrical
conduits

solid
propellant

Tomahawk

Deliveries of Tomahawk Sea Launched Cruise Missiles began in 1983. The missile used is almost identical to the Ground Launched Cruise Missile deployed in Europe by the US Air Force. The US Navy plans to deploy over 4000 SLCM on 190 surface warships and submarines by the mid-1990s. Ships to be fitted include four battleships, seven nuclear-powered cruisers, at least 22 other cruisers and 60 destroyers. Of a total of up to 106 nuclear-powered submarines to be equipped, 36 would have 12 missile tubes built into the pressure hull while the others would carry some cruise missiles instead of some of their normal torpedoes. Seven hundred and fifty-eight of the cruise missiles will carry nuclear warheads with the balance made up of 593 anti-ship missiles with conventional anti-ship warheads and 2643 land attack missiles carrying either 450 kg (1000 lb) high explosive or clusterbomb warheads. The intention is to give most units a capability to attack land targets and to deter nuclear attack on the US Navy by dispersing a nuclear retaliatory capability throughout the fleet, so that no Soviet nuclear attack could destroy the US capability to respond in kind. Among the ships to carry the SLCM will be the four battleships of the Iowa class. These ships have spent most of their careers in reserve, and as well as offering a large well-armoured platform for cruise missiles, their 40.64cm (16") guns are

Specification

GENERAL DYNAMICS BGM 109 SEA LAUNCHED CRUISE MISSILE

Length	6.50 metres (21')
Diameter	53 cm (21")
Weight	1885.5 kg (4190 lb)
Range	nuclear warhead 2780 km (1725 miles) conventional land-attack warhead, submarine launched 925 km (575 miles) conventional land-attack warhead, ship launched 1300 km (805 miles) anti-ship missiles 400 km (250 miles)

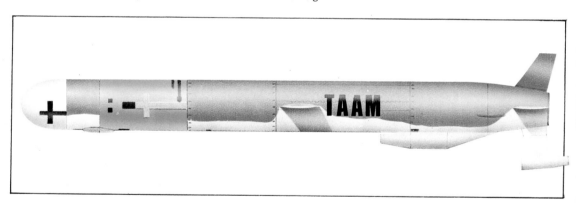

extremely capable in the coastal bombardment role with ranges of up to 23 km (14 miles) possible with shells weighing 990 kg (2200 lbs). The nuclear shells developed for 40.64cm (16") guns in the 1950s have not been available since 1959, but if money was provided, there are a number of suggestions for new conventional shells which could boost the 40.64cm (16") gun's range to beyond 65 km (40 miles) and improve its accuracy and effectiveness. The US Navy is also experimenting with a range of remotely-piloted reconnaissance drones that could be used to target the guns and, in a longer range version, the cruise missiles. In wartime the battleships would be escorted by specialised air defence escorts and would rely on their own electronic defence systems, phalanx anti-missile cannon and 43 cm (17") armour to survive any attackers that succeeded in penetrating the group's outer defences.

Speed	885 kmph (550 mph)
Guidance	Anti-ship missile has active radar guidance to home in on enemy ships. Land attack variants are guided by a terrain comparison system which requires the missile to be fired within 805 km (500 miles) of land so that comparison can be made early enough in flight. The conventional land-attack variants also use a scene-matching system to home in on their target.

Besides SLCM, the US Navy (and the navies of all other nuclear powers) employ a range of other nuclear weapons such as depth charges, aircraft bombs and nuclear-tipped surface-to-air missiles, and is replacing its existing weapons with new ones as they become obsolete. Weapons being developed include the nuclear Standard 2N surface-to-air missile designed to destroy incoming Soviet nuclear missiles. This is designed to destroy nuclear-tipped Soviet anti-ship missiles which might continue to fall towards, and which could still destroy, US ships if their nuclear warheads exploded — even if they were damaged by a conventional anti-missile missile. Other weapons include the Vertical Launched Asroc and submarine launched Sea Lance nuclear-tipped anti-submarine missiles and a new bomb for general and anti-submarine use. These are still thought necessary, particularly as Soviet submarines become harder to detect and harder to destroy by conventional means. The Soviet Navy still places far heavier emphasis on nuclear weapons with up to 50% of its large surface-to-surface missiles armed with nuclear warheads. Over 100 Soviet ships and submarines could operate nuclear anti-ship missiles. The Soviet submarine force also operates nuclear armed anti-submarine missiles, and nuclear torpedoes are carried even by its oldest submarines. It was notable that even an ancient W class conventional submarine which went aground while on a mission in neutral Swedish waters in 1981, was found by the Swedes to be carrying nuclear-tipped torpedoes.

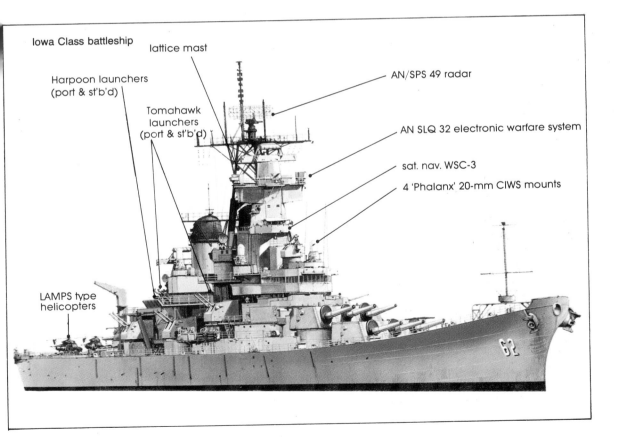

Iowa Class battleship
lattice mast
Harpoon launchers (port & st'b'd)
Tomahawk launchers (port & st'b'd)
AN/SPS 49 radar
AN SLQ 32 electronic warfare system
sat. nav. WSC-3
4 'Phalanx' 20-mm CIWS mounts
LAMPS type helicopters

Pluton / Hades

As well as a strategic force of submarine and land-based ballistic missiles and bombers, France maintains a substantial tactical nuclear force of nuclear armed fighter aircraft and short range ballistic missiles. Hades is intended to replace the current short range missile, the Pluton, from 1992. Hades has more range than Pluton and can hit targets in western Czechoslovakia and south-west East Germany if fired from its French bases. This alleviates the problem with Pluton — that if used, the missile could only explode on West Germany. It does not, however, remove this possibility, as the range is still inadequate to reach East Germany if the missile is fired on any northern arcs. The missile is mobile and its range allows it to be hidden in a large area of eastern France which effectively makes it invulnerable to pre-emptive attack. France has called this nuclear force the "force nucleaire pre-strategique" to convey the impression that it would only be used as a final warning that French strategic nuclear forces were about to be used. The numbers of weapons envisaged, however, (120-180 Hades plus 100 fighters armed with the nuclear-tipped, 80 km (50 mile range) ASMP missile) would themselves pose a great threat to Soviet forces invading Europe, and might be enough to stall an attack before it reached the French border. France is thought to be developing a neutron bomb warhead for Hades which would reduce collateral damage if it were used.

Specification

AÉROSPATIALE PLUTON

Length	7.5 metres (25')
Diameter	65 cm (25.6")
Weight	2400 kg (5340 lb)
Range	120 km (75 miles)
Warhead	1 15-25 kt

AÉROSPATIALE HADES

Length	8 metres (26' 3")
Diameter	60 cm (24")
Weight	N/A
Range	350-400 km (220-250 miles)
Warhead	1 20-60 kt

Pluton

Hades

Lance

Specification

VOUGHT MGM 52C LANCE	
Length	6.5 metres (20')
Diameter	55 cm (22")
Weight	1275-1320 kg (2833-3376 lb) Nuclear/Conventional
Range	120 km (75 miles) [nuclear], 65 km (40 miles) [conventional]
Warhead	1 10 kt nuclear warhead or 450 kg (1000 lb) conventional warhead dispensing 840 bomblets

Lance is the US Army and NATO's current short range ballistic missile system. It is fielded by the armies of the United States, Great Britain, West Germany, Italy, Holland and Belgium with a total of 91 launchers deployed in Europe with an estimated 690 nuclear missiles available. Apart from these NATO powers, the missile has been exported to Israel. Lance can fire either a conventional or a nuclear warhead. The US operates both versions, most of the NATO powers retain Lance solely in the nuclear role using US controlled warheads and Israel operates only the conventional version. Lance is designed to be extremely mobile — normally using its own tracked launcher — but also being air-portable on a light-weight launcher. The impossibility of finding a fairly large number of hidden launchers concealed well behind the immediate frontline is intended to convince an enemy that his army will not be able to escape NATO nuclear retaliation if NATO leaders require this as a response to nuclear or overwhelming conventional attack. Lance also exists in a variant that has been adapted to provide an Enhanced Radiation Warhead (ERW/neutron bomb) capability if NATO leaders decided that this was required. At present this remains only an option and the missiles based in Europe are still armed with a conventional nuclear warhead. Lance will need to be replaced as it gets older, and the US army is currently thinking in terms of a new Corps Support Weapon based on the conventional JCTMS/ACTMS (Joint-Conventional Tactical Missile System/Army Conventional Tactical Missile System) programme and mounted on the launcher now used for the conventional Multiple Launch Rocket System (MLRS). This replacement system would have a longer range, perhaps 250 km (155 miles), so that it could engage targets in the rear of attacking forces.

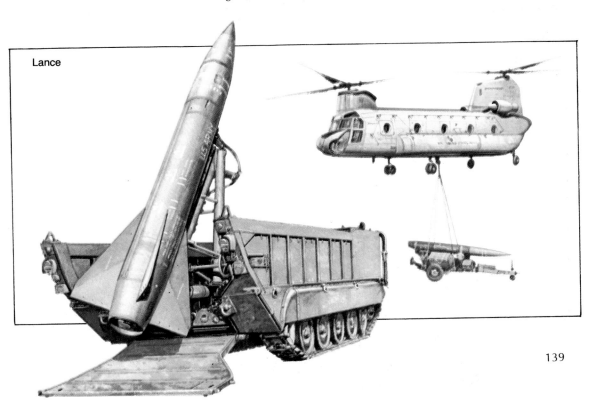

Lance

FROG/SS21

The SS21 is the shortest ranged member of the Soviet Union's family of short ranged ballistic missiles with a range of 120km (75 miles) compared to the 500km (300 miles) range of the SS23 and the 900km (560 miles) range of the SS12 M. The SS21 is replacing the shorter ranged 70km (45 miles) and less accurate, FROG family of missiles which are deployed with four launchers assigned to each Soviet Army division. By 1987 the Soviets had deployed around 130 SS21 launchers with 760 of the FROGs still in service. This is the total of launchers rather than missiles, as it is assumed that, like the West with its far smaller number of launchers, the Soviet Army has more than one missile per launcher. There are no reliable estimates available of just how many missiles exist. Like FROG, the SS21 is presumed to have a range of nuclear, chemical and conventional warheads available to it. Unlike the unguided FROG, the SS2l is believed to have the accuracy to be useful in a conventional role, attacking targets near the frontline like supply depots, troop concentrations, forward airfields and command posts. There is also a fear that it could be used to destroy NATO's Early Warning Radars and Surface to Air Missile sites which are all deployed near the inter-German border. Once these were knocked out, Warsaw Pact aircraft would find it far easier to penetrate into NATO's airspace to attack its rear areas. The Soviets may have deployed a cluster-bomb warhead for the SS21 which would make it especially effective in any of these roles.

Specification

FROG

Length	9 metres (29' 10")
Diameter	55cm (22")
Weight	2282 kg (5070 lb)
Range	65-72 km (40-45 miles)
Accuracy	400 metres (1300') CEP
Warhead	HE 450 kg 1200 kt/1,000

SS21

Length	9.5 metres (31')
Diameter	45cm (18")
Weight	2970 kg (6600 lb)
Range	100-120 km (60-75 miles)
Accuracy	300 metres (980') CEP
Warhead	450 kg (1100 kt/1,000 lb) Conventiona

FROG-7

M 110

The M 110 has been in service with the US Army and most other NATO armies since 1962. In 1986 the US Army had 1050 guns with the NATO allies fielding another 370. The M 110 has a conventional role and can be equipped with a range of conventional, bomblet-dispensing and rocket-assisted long-range shells, but it also has a nuclear role. The importance of this lies in the fact that the nuclear shells for the M 110 are among NATO's least vulnerable nuclear weapons. Unlike fixed targets like fighter airfields, the M 110 gun is designed to be mobile and to hide on the battlefield, and there are so many guns available to fire the shell that the task of trying to destroy every opposing nuclear delivery system becomes impossible. Although such short-ranged systems are criticised because they could only be used on NATO's own territory, this may be offset by the fact that, if they were used, they would destroy the Soviet army itself: a prospect which is very likely to deter Soviet army commanders. There are estimated to be around 2600 nuclear shells for the M 110 - some operated under dualkey by allied forces. The US Army also has nuclear shells available for its M 109, 155mm, self-propelled guns. ERW (neutron bomb) shells have been developed for both weapons and some shells have been converted to give this option if needed. No ERW shells have yet been deployed in Europe. Since the late 1970s the Soviet army has invested heavily in new artillery which also has a nuclear capability and may now have more weapons in this category than the West. The Soviet equivalent of the M 110 is called the 2 S7. This is only one of a new family of nuclear-capable, self-propelled guns and mortars with calibres ranging from 155 to 240 mm.

Specification

M 110 A2 203mm Self Propelled Howitzer

Weight of gun	29,250 kg (65,000 lb)
Range	16.7-29 km (10.4-18 miles)
Weight of nuclear shell	118.8 kg (264 lb)
Warhead	1 5-10 kt

M 110 8in SP Howitzer

A FROG 7 missile on its mobile launcher. FROG is being replaced by the SS21 but still makes up the majority of the Soviet battlefield missile force.

Conclusion

The foregoing pages have illustrated the many types of weapon that can be built around nuclear explosions and how deeply such weapons are embedded in the strategic scene. Chiefly in the hands of the Superpowers and a very few lesser actors, the central nuclear balance directly or indirectly affects most other military confrontations in the modern world. Despite recent talk by some political leaders of "removing the threat of nuclear weapons", talk reminiscent of the rhetoric of "General and Complete Disarmament" in the days of Khruschev and Kennedy, it seems highly unlikely that nuclear weapons will disappear. Even if they did so, the knowledge of how to make them cannot be forgotten and consequently their potential reappearance could never be ruled out. Moreover, there must be considerable doubt as to whether the complete removal of such a fundamental strategic factor could be attempted without running the risk of great and conceivably disastrous instability.

So far the main arena for the development of nuclear strategic doctrine and for the proliferation of weapons has been the East-West confrontation organised around the two Superpowers. It is this confrontation which has so far provided the most obvious context for a major nuclear conflict, though the *casus belli* might well arise not in the most elaborately prepared battleground, Europe, but in some "third area" such as the Middle and Far East. The nuclear armament of China and soon perhaps of such other countries as Israel, India or Pakistan foreshadow the prospect of other and possibly more volatile patterns of nuclear conflict than the by now highly structured framework of Soviet-American deterrence.

In Europe, hitherto the main fulcrum of the nuclear balance, NATO has made repeated efforts to break away from excessive dependence on nuclear weapons, but has so far never succeeded. As we have seen there are two interrelated reasons for this: first, political unwillingness to afford the wherewithal for a full conventional counterbalance to the forces of the Warsaw Pact and, second, doubt if it would really be wise to do so and to renounce the qualitatively different aura of nuclear weapons. Thus in evolving its strategy from Massive Retaliation to Flexible Response, NATO has not done more than relegate nuclear weapons to the second line of defence and continue to rely heavily on the hope that, looming in the background, nuclear weapons can thereby remain the first line of deterrence against war breaking out.

Throughout the nuclear age there has been a debate between those who consciously or not lean to one or other of two hypothetical extremes; between those who believe the task is to take nuclear weapons out of the strategic equation and deal with conflict by other means and those who believe that this is either impossible or undesirable and think we must build nuclear weapons into strategies and profit from the caution they induce. The first tendency, whether to be achieved by disarmament or strategies such as Massive Assured Destruction, which are clearly disproportionate to actual political issues, is criticised for "making the world safe for a conventional war" and for failing catastrophically if fail it does. The second tendency is criticised

TRI

F15E

Ranger   Barmine layer

AH64

E8

Tornado

Aquila

F15E

F4G

copperhead shell

F15E

Forward
observer vehicle

A10

M109

ACTMS

143

for making the world safe for nuclear war and offering no guarantee that the intended limitations will be observed. Something of both tendencies can be seen in the current debate over Starwars, some seeing strategic defence as removing the threat of nuclear weapons and thus returning the world to dependence on conventional weapons, others anticipating less than perfect defences being part of the apparatus for limiting the consequences of nuclear war. Technological limitations make it seem likely that only the second role for strategic defences will become a practicable option in this century.

It is clear that one of the objections to trying to do without nuclear weapons is that they solve some of the problems of those who would otherwise face daunting conventional threats. The European members of NATO, as the immediate neighbours of one of the two greatest military powers in the world, face this dilemma in the most acute form. As a result the alliance has seen repeated efforts to see whether a satisfactory conventional alternative to nuclear deterrence can be provided.

In recent years great technological advances have created much so-called "emerging" or "new weapon" technology (ET or NWT). Optimists believe that such weapons could compensate for nuclear weapons in two related ways: first enhancing the overall effectiveness of conventional defence so that its obvious ability to stop an offensive could serve as a deterrent to aggression as reliable as nuclear weapons; and, second, substitute for nuclear weapons in executing many specific military tasks hitherto thought beyond the bounds of practicability.

Thus new accuracy in delivery systems coupled with much more efficient warheads, such as shaped charges against armour and full-air explosives against troop concentrations, offers much greater effectiveness against the modern all-arms attack centred round the tank. To supplement such potential on the forward battlefield, accuracy at longer ranges opens up the possibility of attacking targets such as airfields and logistic chokepoints. Used in the so-called Follow-on-Forces-Attack, such technology could go some way to eliminate the need to compensate for inaccuracy and poor target location by using nuclear weapons, incidentally permitting such action with less probable political agonising than would be occasioned by nuclear release. Such capabilities might even go some way to replicate one of the most significant defensive effects of nuclear weapons: the imposition of dispersal on offensive formations.

It would be wise, however, to qualify the more optimistic forecasts for NWT. Many of the proposed capabilities are still unproven, numerous systems have failed in development and all are expensive. This is particularly true of the longer range capabilities which are the ones most relevant to displacing hitherto preferred nuclear roles. Moreover the risks posed to an aggressor by conventional weapons are probably qualitatively different from those presented by nuclear weapons both in the primary threat to his forces and their secondary significance for the prospects of escalation. Nuclear weapons will also still be necessary to deter enemy first use, unless complete nuclear disarmament is achieved.

P. 142 An impression of some of the many applications of emerging conventional technology to the ground war in Europe. Airborne sensors look deep into enemy rear-areas, from aircraft like the TR1 shown and the projected E8 J STARS aircraft. These are supplemented by sensors on small drone aircraft that penetrate enemy airspace. Tornado and F15E aircraft attack airfields with stand-off missiles carrying specialised runway-destroying munitions. Similar attacks are made on chokepoints in enemy logistical services. These missions may be supplemented by tactical ballistic missiles such as the ACTMS shown. These long range technologies are not yet all perfected and location remains a problem for mobile targets.

Meanwhile in the forward battle area several types of smart weapon, mostly now available or in advanced development, attack the first enemy echelon. A10 tank-buster aircraft are assisted by AH64 anti-tank helicopters, by homing artillery munitions guided by forward laser designators, and by multiple-rocket-launched smart submunitions. New methods of rapidly deploying anti-tank mines prepare further hazards.

Right: Space has become a vital area for deploying military facilities. Intelligence, reconnaissance, communication and control functions are already very dependent on space vehicles and both superpowers are developing the capability to attack such facilities. Given their importance the military pay-off for such attacks could be great but, on the other hand, there are considerable hazards, some arising from the loss of one's own facilities and others from the possible danger that depriving the enemy of the ability to monitor and control the battle may cause him to behave rashly. The failure of the American space shuttle and the Soviet advances toward constructing permanently manned space stations have drawn attention to the new dimensions of space activity that may soon become possible once large installations can be constructed. Space is certain to remain a major strategic asset from now on so far as information functions are concerned; it remains to be seen whether tacit or negotiated arms control can prevent it becoming an arena for combat.

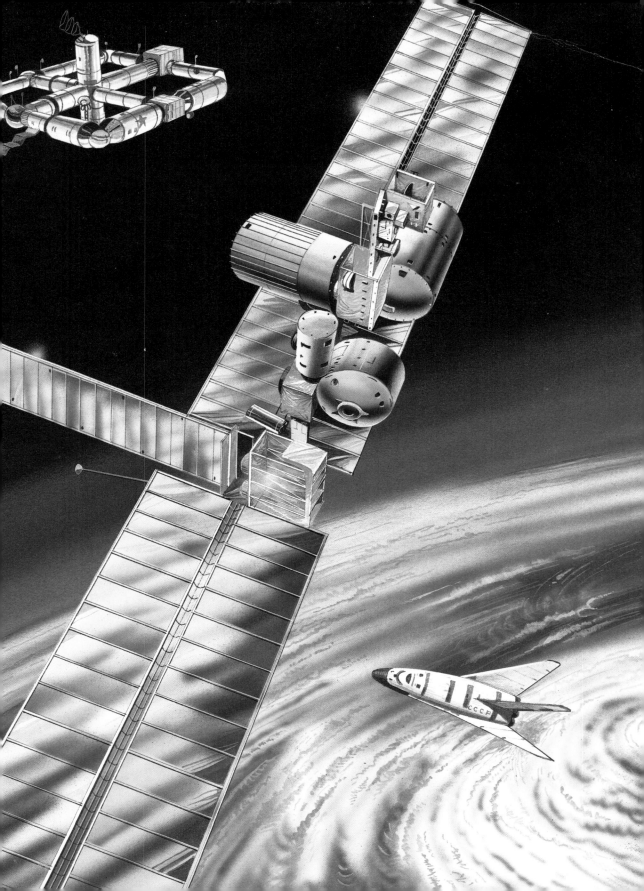

On the other hand, nuclear weapons for use on the battlefield, once regarded as among the "safer" modes of nuclear war, are now generally viewed with considerable misgiving. Relatively ineffective unless used in large numbers, they threaten a quickly devastated, confused and uncontrollable battlefield. Deeper but fewer strikes on airfields and logistics might offer military effectiveness with more controllability, but even here it seems clear that earlier notions of limited nuclear war were "over optimistic" and that such uses if they occur would have to be severely constrained in numbers of weapons and types of target if the political and technical bounds of restraint were not to be breached. Similarly, at the strategic level, any use of nuclear weapons to back-up extended deterrence would have to be extremely limited if there were to be a reasonable chance of control and therefore of political credibility. Nevertheless, because any nuclear power with a monopoly of capability for limited nuclear strikes backed up by a capacity for "assured destruction", might just believe it could get away with the former while deterring all-out retaliation by its less flexible opponent, a strategic deterrent probably requires *some* capability for limited or so-called "modulated" strikes.

The most rational future for nuclear strategy at both the theatre and strategic levels is thus probably the continued maintenance of deterrent forces with a capability for limited action, even though we must admit that if such action begins, the best hopes of nuclear deterrence will have failed and the world will have reached a desperate plight. Forces for such strategies could be much more modest than those hitherto prepared under a muddled mixture of "war fighting" and "assured destruction" thinking. Negotiated arms control could play a constructive part in achieving such reductions and this seems a more promising way forward than more utopian schemes to abolish nuclear weapons.

The technological and doctrinal wherewithal for such a world of more moderate deterrence can be seen emerging on the contemporary strategic scene, mixed up with a good deal of other, counterproductive development. To make progress possible will require an effort to refine and make more explicit sound nuclear strategic doctrine and then the political courage to define the minimal forces necessary to implement it. This would provide an irreducible floor above which the surplus could be negotiated away without endangering security. Thus coherent strategic doctrine and adequate forces are not an obstacle to successful arms control but the only sound basis for it.

Right: Prospects for space-based laser guns to intercept missiles in the boost phase provided one of the most science fiction-like aspects of ABM technology but technological difficulties, particularly the problem of getting the necessary energy sources into position, make this now seem a possibility for the next century, if at all.

Glossary

A

AABNCP	Advanced Airborne National Command Post
AAM	Air-to-Air Missile
ABM	Anti-Ballistic Missile
ABM Treaty	Treaty between the US and the Soviet Union limiting Anti-Ballistic Missile Systems (1972).
ABRV	Advanced Ballistic Re-entry Vehicle
Active Homing	Autonomous means by which a missile seeks its target. Principally by means of emitting a signal e.g. acoustic or radar, which when reflected by a target is detected by a receiver in the missile homing guidance system. The reflected signal provides the information necessary for the missile guidance to direct the course of the missile to the target.
ACTMS	Army Conventional Tactical Missile System
AEC	Atomic Energy Commission (United States) now part of the Department of Energy.
AFAP	Artillery Fired Atomic Projectiles
AFBMD	Air Force Ballistic Missile Division (United States)
AFF	Arming, Fusing and Firing System
AGR	Advanced Gas-cooled Reactor
Air-burst	The term for the detonation of a weapon in the atmosphere above a target at a pre-set altitude to maximise the destructive effective effect.
AIRS	Advanced Inertial Reference System
ALBM	Air-Launched Ballistic Missile
ALCM	Air-Launched Cruise Missile
Anti-Radar	Weapons designed to suppress radar installations.
Apogee	The highest point of a trajectory or orbit.
ASATS	Anti-Satellite Systems
ASDC	Alternate Space Defense Centre
ASROC	Anti-Submarine Rocket
ASW	Anti-Submarine Warfare
ATB	Advanced Technology Bomber – The US B2 Stealth bomber.
ATBM	Anti-Tactical Ballistic Missile (missile or system) weapons designed to intercept tactical ballistic missiles like the Soviet SS23.
ATF	Advanced Tactical Fighter
Avionics	The electronic equipment fit for an aircraft.
AWACS	Airborne Warning and Control System

B

B–	Designation for bomber aircraft, Soviet aircraft identified as bombers are designated with NATO codenames the first letter of which corresponds to the classification of the system, e.g. for bombers: Badger, Bear, Blinder, Backfire, Blackjack, etc.
Big Bird	Generic name for a series of US spy satellites.
BMD	Ballistic Missile Defence/Defense – system designed to defend against ballistic missiles.
BMEWS	Ballistic Missile Early Warning System
Booster	Term generally given to the first propulsion stage of a ballistic missile providing the initial acceleration for the missile flight.
Bus	See MIRV Bus.
BWE	Boiling Water Reactor. A nuclear reactor in which the nuclear fuel boils water circulating around the fuel rods, the steam thus created driving the turbines which generate electricity.

C

C3	Command, Control and Communications
C³I	Command, Control, Communications and Intelligence
CADIN/Pinetree Line	Aircraft detection radar network in southern Canada.
CANDU	Canadian Deuterium Uranium reactor
Cat House	Intermediate-range Soviet radar, associated with the defence of Moscow.
CBW	Chemical, Biological Warfare
CEP	Circular Error Probable, a measure of the accuracy attributable to ballistic missiles. It is the radius of circle into which fifty per cent of the warheads aimed at the centre of the circle are predicted to fall.

Chaff	Radar reflective material sometimes comprised of fine wire pieces cut to fractions of the wavelength of the radars to be jammed. Chaff operates by obscuring the target from the detecting radar by creating a much larger radar signature due to the reflectivity of the chaff material.
Chain Reaction	A chain reaction results when a mass of fissile material is brought together so that sustained fission occurs as in a nuclear explosion.
CIA	Central Intelligence Agency (United States)
CIWS	Close-In Weapon Systems
CMP	Counter Military Potential. A measure of the potential capability of a nuclear weapon to destroy hard targets, e.g. where the accuracy of the delivery system has special significance.
CND	Campaign for Nuclear Disarmament
Cold Launch	A technique by which a missile is ejected from its silo by compressed air, after which the rocket motor is ignited. The technique slightly enhances the throw-weight of the missile and enables the silo to be reused.
Command Guidance	Control of a missile's flight by commands from ground stations transmitted to the missile by radio signals.
Conventional	Not nuclear, i.e. Chemical high explosive.
Cosmos	Generic name for a series of Soviet satellites some of which are spy satellites.
Countermeasures	Measures undertaken by a defender to reduce or eliminate the effectiveness of a weapon system.
Critical Mass	The amount of fissile material needed to be brought together in order to sustain a chain reaction.
Cruise Missile	A missile which flies supported by wing or body lift.
CTBT	Comprehensive nuclear Test Ban Treaty

D

Damage Radius	The radius of a circle from the centre of which the destructive effects over distance are measured for specific weapons.
DARPA	Defence Advanced Research Projects Agency (United States)
DCS	Defense Communications Systems
Decoy	Carried as a penetration aid by the MIRV Bus of a missile in order to allow the warheads to reach their targets without interference. Can include decoy warheads and chaff.
Decoy Warhead	A replica of some characteristics of a true ballistic missile re-entry vehicle such as a radar cross section.
Depressed Trajectory	A ballistic trajectory with an abnormally low apogee to reduce the possibility of early detection by radars. Use of such trajectories has the effect of reducing the range of the missile.
Deuterium	Thermonuclear fuel, together with such substances as deuterium-tritium mixture and lithium deuteride. Can be used in various combinations to tailor the type of nuclear blast to the particular target. Deuterium is also a constituent of heavy water.
DEW	Directed Energy Weapon. Weapon that destroys its target by focusing energy rays upon it rather than by impact or explosive effects.
DEW Line	Distant Early Warning Line detection radars
Discoverer	Series of early US satellites that were the precursors to the first photo-reconnaissance satellites.
Dog House	Intermediate-range Soviet radar, associated with Moscow defence.
DSCS	Defense Satellite Communications Systems
DSMAC	Digital Scene-Matching Area Correlation
DSP	Defense Support Program. Project designation for a series of US early warning satellites.
Dual-Key System	Physical system to assure two or more nations control over final decision to use nuclear weapons during time of war. This allows for consultation among allies on the decision to resort to a nuclear attack.

E

ECCM	Electronic Counter Countermeasures. A range of measures that can be implemented to counteract or reduce the effectiveness of ECM by improving the resistance of radars to jamming, for example.
ECM	Electronic Countermeasures. A range of electronic and other measures (e.g. chaff) used to reduce the effectiveness of enemy electronic systems, primarily radars, missile guidance systems and communications and surveillance systems.
Electron Class	Soviet class of satellites aimed at providing coverage of the continental United States.

	ELF	Extremely Low Frequency. Frequencies used for communication with submerged submarines.
	ELINT	Electronic Intelligence. Refers to detailed information of the characteristics of electronic equipment obtained by means such as monitoring radar transmissions of enemy surface to air missile sites.
	EMP	Electromagnetic Pulse. The pulse of intense electromagnetic radiation emitted by a nuclear explosion.
	EMT	Equivalent megatonnage: A measure of the effect of nuclear weapons against area targets such as cities or industrial complexes.
	Endo-Atmospheric	Normally used with reference to ABMs designed to intercept ballistic missile re-entry vehicles after they have entered the Earth's atmosphere.
	Enhanced Radiation	A nuclear weapon whose design maximises the generation of radiation effects over those of blast and heat.
	Enrichment	A process capable of increasing the content of Uranium 235 to a higher level than that found in natural uranium, useful for either nuclear reactors or nuclear weapons.
	ET	Emerging Technology. New high technology, using the products of the microelectronics revolution which, when applied to weapons, may bring a major leap in capabilities. The impact on conventional forces may be particularly marked.
	EUCOM	United States European Command
	Exo-Atmospheric	Referring to ABM intercepts outside the Earth's atmosphere.
F	FAE	Fuel/Air Explosive. A weapon which disperses fuel into the atmosphere above a target prior to detonation. The combustion of the fuel/air mixture creates intense blast and heat.
	FBM	Fleet Ballistic Missile (United States)
	FBR	Fast Breeder Reactor
	Ferret Satellite	A satellite collecting electronic intelligence.
	Fin Stabilised	Missiles whose stability in flight is maintained by aerodynamic control surfaces or fins.
	Fireball	The massive, bright, hot spherical mass created immediately after the initial detonation of a nuclear device. As the hot gases within it expand, the fireball moves upwards later forming a mushroom cloud.
	Fissile Material	Either uranium or plutonium that is in a form that can be utilised in nuclear reactors or nuclear weapons. Fissile material for nuclear weapons is referred to as 'weapons grade'.
	Flaming Arrow	American satellite communications link for nuclear command and control.
	Flight Profile	The flight path of an aircraft as a function of its altitude at the beginning, middle and end of its flight to target, i.e. High, High, High (abbreviated to HI HI HI) or similarly High Low Low (HI LO LO).
	FNS	Force Nucleaire Strategique. French Strategic Nuclear Force originally known as the Force de Frappe.
	FOBS	Fractional Orbital Bombardment Systems. A method of ballistic missile attack over intercontinental distances that involves launching the warhead into a fractional orbit around the Earth so that the warhead arrives over the target from the opposite direction of a direct ballistic trajectory.
	FOFA	Follow On Forces Attack. NATO concept for targeting Soviet rear echelons to prevent them from reaching the front and over-running NATO forces that would be already occupied dealing with the first echelon of the Soviet attack.
	Force de Frappe	The French independent nuclear deterrent.
	Force Ratio	The ratio of comparable weapon systems in the arsenals of opposing forces.
	Free-Fall Weapons	Air-delivered bombs without their own guidance system.
	FROG	Free-flight Rocket Over Ground. A rocket without specialised guidance, whose ballistic trajectory is determined by its pre-launch elevation and azimuth.
G	GCR	Gas-Cooled Reactor
	GEMINI	A series of American manned spaceflights.
	Geo-Synchronous	Orbits of satellites whose position over a given point on the Equator remains the same by synchronisation of the satellite's orbit with the rotation of the Earth.
	GIUK	Greenland-Iceland-UK Gap
	GLCM	Ground Launched Cruise Missile
	GPS	Global Positioning System. A system of American navigational satellites.
	Ground Zero	The point on the Earth over which a nuclear weapon is detonated.

	GWEN	Ground Wave Emergency Network. System for providing reliable communications with land based US strategic forces. GWEN depends on a large number of dispersed radio relay transmitters to provide redundancy and ensure that messages can get through even in a nuclear attack.

H

Hard Target	A target protected against the blast, heat and radiation of nuclear explosions : for example, a missile silo.
HE	High Explosive
Heavy Water	Deuterium oxide: water containing a high proportion of the hydrogen isotope, deuterium. Used as a coolant in HWRs.
Hen	A long-range Soviet radar providing warning of ICBM attack.
HF	High Frequency
HOE	Homing Overlay Experiment. An anti-ballistic missile system experiment.
Homing	Guided towards a target by onboard guidance system.
Hot Launch	Launch method for ballistic missiles involving ignition of motors while missile is in silo. The method precludes reuse of the silo for another missile until the silo is repaired.
Howitzer	A weapon designed to fire shells on a higher trajectory than normal guns and at a lower velocity.
HWR	Heavy Water Reactor
Hypersonic	Velocities many times the speed of sound, e.g. Mach 4 and above.

I

IAEA	International Atomic Energy Agency
ICBM	Intercontinental Ballistic Missile
IGS	Inertial Guidance System
Inertial Guidance	An onboard guidance system, based on precise measurement of the accelerations experienced by a vehicle.
INF	Intermediate Range Nuclear Forces
IR	Infra-Red
IRBM	Intermediate Range Ballistic Missiles

J

Jamming	Disrupting or confusing an enemy's communications, radars and allied equipment.
JCTMS	Joint Conventional Tactical Missile. Joint US army and airforce project for a conventional ballistic missile equipped with smart warheads to attack Soviet armour and support columns at long range. JCTMS may finally emerge as separate army and airforce programmes.
JSS	Joint Surveillance System (United States)
JSTARS	Joint Surveillance Targeting and Reconnaissance System. Joint US army/ airforce system using high flying (RT1, C18/ E8 and possible 'stealth' successors) to locate moving targets 400 km (250 miles) behind the front line. JSTARS data would be used to target missiles like the JCTMS.

K

Killing Grounds or Zone	Area where weapons are expected to come under attack or troops exposed to fire.
KKV	Kinetic Kill Vehicle. Anti-ballistic missile/warhead missile relying on its momentum rather than an explosive warhead to destroy its target.
Kt	Kiloton. An explosive yield equal to 1000 tons of TNT.

L

LAMPS	Light Airborne Multi-Purpose System. Anti-submarine helicopter equipment, which can comprise search radar, sonar buoy and MAD equipment, plus electronic support machinery. The helicopter so equipped can also have an attack capability.
Launch-Under-Attack Policy	A policy of launching missiles under attack conditions to prevent a large number of them being destroyed in their silos.
LCC	Launch Control Centre. The supporting vehicle for a cruise missile TEL, providing launch capability for the missiles.
LF	Low Frequency
LNO	Limited Nuclear Options
Look-down Radar	Aircraft radar with the ability to distinguish from above airborne targets from the ground clutter produced by the Earth's surface. Cruise missiles are capable of being detected in this way.
Low Level Penetration	Flight profile of aircraft designed to minimise detection by ground based radars.
LRBM	Long Range Ballistic Missile
LRTNF	Long Range Theatre Nuclear Forces

	LWR	Light Water Reactor. The most commonly used nuclear reactor, employing water to prevent the uranium fuel from overheating; can be one of two kinds, either the Boiling Water Reactor, or the Pressurised Water Reactor.
M	MAD	Magnetic Anomoly Detection system. Used to detect submerged submarines, a MAD receiver is carried over the sea, for example by an aircraft, and is designed to detect the very small change in the Earth's local magnetic field caused by the submarine.
	MAD	Mutual Assured Destruction. Idea of deterrent consisting in the destruction of a large part of the civilian population and industrial capacity of a country as retaliation. A policy expressed for a time by the United States.
	Main Operating Base	The normal location of an aircraft or GLCM. The latter would be moved to its operational deployment area in time of conflict.
	MaRV	Manoeuvrable Re-entry Vehicle.
	MAS	Mutually Assured Survival. A concept in which mutual survival is made possible by the deployment of strategic defences rather than by dependence on the ability to retaliate. Survival, however, would only be possible if defences were totally effective otherwise survival would mean death for millions.
	MBFR	Mutual and Balanced Force Reductions
	Mikoyan-Gurevich (MiG)	Soviet designer and manufacturer of combat aircraft.
	Millisecond	One-thousandth of a second.
	Milstar	A series of two-way communications satellites, due for full-scale operation by the late 1980s and including the possibility of unjammable communications.
	MIRV	Multiple Independently Targetable Re-entry Vehicle
	MIRV Bus	Post boost vehicle which carries MIRV warheads and aims and releases them at their targets.
	MLF	Multi-Lateral Force. A scheme for collective nuclear forces.
	Mt	Megaton. The yield of a nuclear weapon, equivalent to 1,000,000 tons of TNT.
	MSBS	Mer-Sol-Ballistique Strategique. French term for an SLBM.
	MX	Missile Experimental. The new US ICBM subsequently named as the MGM 118 Peacekeeper.
N	National Military Command System	The centre of the World-wide US Military Command and Control System, providing the necessary information and support for the NCA to make executive decisions regarding the direction of US strategic forces.
	NATO	North Atlantic Treaty Organization. Created by Treaty, 1949, now comprising sixteen countries in Europe and North America, guaranteeing mutual assistance and military co-operation. The Warsaw Pact arose in large part as a response to German entry into NATO, 1954.
	Navstar	Satellite component of the US Global Positioning System (GPS).
	NBC	Nuclear, Biological and Chemical. An NBC suit is available for issue to infantry and other fighting men, in the event of any of these three weapon types on the battlefield.
	NCA	National Command Authority. The main security officials of any country. In the United States, this consists of the President, together with his senior political and military decision-makers.
	NORAD	North American Air Defence Command. The combined US and Canadian command responsible for world-wide surveillance and early warning of air attack on North America by nuclear or conventional means.
	NPT	Non-Proliferation Treaty
	Nuclear Artillery Pieces	Guns capable of firing nuclear armed shells.
	Nuclear Burst	The detonation of a nuclear weapon, sometimes referred to as a nuclear Air-Burst when the weapon is detonated at a pre-set distance above the ground.
	NWT	New Weapons Technology
O	OTH	Over the Horizon (Radar). Long Range 800 – 2900 km (500 – 1800 mile) radar for detection of air and and cruise missile threats.
	Overkill	The building-up of more weapons than would theoretically be adequate to destroy all specified targets. This ensures that sufficient back-up is allowed for in the event of some weapons failing to function correctly and thus not destroying their targets.
P	PACBAR	Pacific Radar Barrier (United States). Designed to give space surveillance coverage over the Pacific.

PAL	Permissive Action Links. System of mechanical and code locks designed to prevent any nuclear weapon being exploded by unauthorised persons.
PARCS	Perimeter Acquisition Radar attack Characterization System (United States)
Pave Paws	A radar system providing warning of a sea-launched ballistic missile attack from either the East Coast or the West Coast against the continental United States.
Payload	Total mass of a missile's warheads, together with their associated arming fuzing and safety systems, penetration aids, and any other device which is carried to the target.
PBPS	Post-Boost Propulsion System
PBW	Particle Beam Weapon
Penetration Aids	Carried by the Bus containing the warheads of an ICBM these include decoys and ECM intended to deceive detecting radars and ABMs in order to allow the missile's warheads to reach their targets without interference.
PNET	Peaceful Nuclear Explosions Treaty
Point Target	A target small enough to be indentified by a single co-ordinate on operational maps: for example, a missile silo.
Pre-emptive Attack	An assault started on the basis of evidence that an enemy attack is about to take place.
PSI	Pounds per Square Inch. Measure of blast overpressure caused by a nuclear weapon. Five PSI would destroy the average house and severely damage tower blocks. A missile silo could withstand 2000-5000 PSI.
PTBT	Partial Test Ban Treaty
PWR	Pressurised Water Reactor. A nuclear reactor in which water is circulated around the fuel at very high pressure to prevent boiling. This water heats a separate circuit to produce steam for turbines.

Q

QRA	Quick Reaction Alert

R

RADAG	Radar Area Guidance system as in the US Pershing II missile.
Radar Cross-Section	The radar picture created by radar waves reflected back from a given target surface. The image so produced is influenced partly, but not wholly, by size: structural shape can also play an important part, as can the reflecting characteristics of the materials from which the target is made.
Real Time	Something instantaneous rather than delayed in transmission, as in communications or reconnaissance.
Re-entry	The act of re-entering the Earth's atmosphere during the flight of a ballistic missile.
Regional Operations Control Centre	One of seven control centres of the JSS, receiving information of intruding aircraft in North America from radar locations.
Rhyolite	A class of US satellite, designed to provide early warning of Soviet ICBM tests and launches.
RV	Re-entry Vehicle

S

SAC	Strategic Air Command (United States). The US Air Force Command responsible for America's manned strategic bombers and ICBMs.
SACEUR	Supreme Allied Commander Europe
SALT	Strategic Arms Limitations Talks. Negotiations between the Soviet Union and the US, aimed to halt the expansion of strategic weapon systems of both countries, with the possibility of reducing these forces.
SAM	Surface-to-Air Missile
SAMOS	US spy satellite using radio link with Earth to transmit reconnaissance photographs.
Satellite Link	Space based links designed to supplement earth-based communications links: an example is Flaming Arrow, with back-up communications for GLCM units when deployed away from their Main Operating Base.
SDI	Strategic Defense Initiative. US Research and development programme for strategic defences; organisation established after President Reagan's 1983 'Star Wars' speech.
SHAPE	Supreme Headquarters Allied Powers in Europe
SHF	Super High Frequency. Can be used, for example, for communications with satellites.
Short Range ballistic missile	Missile with a range of 500-1000 km (310-620 miles). New subdivision created by need to encompass missiles like the SS23 and SS12 in the current arms control talks. Missiles like the SS21 and Scud are now referred to as shorter

		range weapons.
Shroud		The uppermost part of a missile, protecting the warheads and RV.
SICBM		Small ICBM. The US projected lightweight mobile ICBM also known as 'Midgetman'.
Silo		The underground base of a nuclear missile, with facilities for the missile's launch. The silo provides protection from nuclear attack, and often a high-precision attack is the only means of destroying it.
SINS		Ships Inertial Navigation System
SIOP		Single Integrated Operations Plan. US plan for strategic retaliatory strike in the event of nuclear war, including targets, tactics and force strength needed for such a plan.
SIRE		Space Infrared Sensor
SLBM		Submarine/Sea-Launched Ballistic Missile
SLCM		Sea Launched Cruise Missile
SMW		Strategic Missile Wing (United States)
SNLE		Sous-marine Nucleaire Lance-Engins. French nuclear missile submarines able to carry the MSBS.
Soft Target		A target unprotected against the blast, heat and radiation of a nuclear explosion, such as a major centre of population.
Sonar Buoy		A buoy equipped with sonar equipment designed to detect submerged submarines, that listens for sounds reflected back from the submarine.
SOSUS		Sound Surveillance System
SPADATS		Space Surveillance System (United States)
SPADOC		Space Defence Operations Centre (United States)
Special Ammunition Storage		Storage for nuclear warheads, particularly those of tactical weapons; an example is the US Lance tactical missile used by several NATO countries, with warheads under joint control by US and allied custodians.
SRAM		Short-Range Attack Missile. An air-launched nuclear-tipped missile.
SS		Designation applied to Soviet nuclear missiles.
SS		Submersible Ship. Submarine (conventionally powered).
SSB		Submarine armed with ballistic missiles (conventionally powered).
SSBN		Submarine armed with ballistic missiles and nuclear powered – a submarine with a strategic nuclear deterrence role like the US Ohio, Soviet Typhoon and British Resolution classes.
SSBS		Sol-Sol-Ballistique-Strategique. French term for IRBM.
SSG		Submarine, conventionally powered and armed with guided cruise missiles, usually anti-ship but in some cases with a strategic role.
SSGN		A guided missile armed submarine, as above, but with nuclear propulsion, e.g the Soviet Oscar class.
SS-N		Designation applied to Soviet sea-launched nuclear missiles.
SSN		A nuclear powered submarine not armed with ballistic or guided missiles. Often referred to as hunter-killer submarine reflecting its ASW role. The distinction between SSN and SSGN has become unclear as most British, US and French SSN now carry anti-ship missiles in their torpedo tubes and US and Soviet SSN now carry various long range cruise missiles. SSGN is usually now used only to designate submarines that are designed to function as missile platforms, whilst multi-purpose submarines are still designated as SSN.
Stand-Off Bomb		A weapon fired by a manned aircraft some distance from the target, and capable of reaching the target under its own power. This allows the aircraft to stand off from the target, thus avoiding its defences.
START		Strategic Arms Reduction Talks
Stealth		Technique for reducing the visibility of aircraft on radar using shapes and materials to reduce reflectivity.
SUBROC		US submarine-launched missile, essentially a rocket propelled nuclear depth charge designed to destroy submarines.
Sukhoi		Soviet designer and manufacturer of combat aircraft.
Swing-Wing		Aircraft designed with variable geometry wings. The main portions of the wings are hinged, and can extend for subsonic flight, while being capable of being folded back to allow supersonic dash.
T TACAMO		Take Command And Move Out. US Navy means of communicating with submerged submarines when necessary by means of specially-equipped communications aircraft.
Tactical Aircraft		Land and Carrier based aircraft capable of carrying out a variety of roles

especially in and around the battlefield. This can include the carrying of tactical nuclear weapons.

TAINS	Terrain-comparison Aided Inertial Navigation System
Tall King	Series of Soviet intermediate-range aircraft-detection and tracking radars.
Teeth to Tail Radio	The ratio of fighting men (Teeth) to the logistical support personnel and hence non-fighting men (Tail) or armies, especially when deployed in an operational area.
TEL	Transporter Erector Launcher. The combined transporting vehicle and launch platform for a GLCM.
Thermonuclear Warhead	The hydrogen warhead commonly known as the H-bomb, which has a much greater power than the earlier atomic weapons.
Throw Weight	A ballistic missile's payload capacity: expressed in terms of the RV, its warhead(s), and associated devices such as arming and fuzing systems, and penetration aids.
TNT	TriNitroToluene. A high explosive, often used as an equivalent measure of the yield of nuclear warheads.
TTBT	Threshold Test Ban Treaty
Tupolev	Soviet designer and manufacturer of combat aircraft, mainly bombers.
Turbofan Engine	A later powerplant than the earlier turbojet engine, a major advance being its requirement for less fuel. Turbofan engines can thus help provide greater range.

U
UHF	Ultra High Frequency
US	United States

V
Vela Hotel	US series of satellites launched to detect nuclear explosions.
VHF	Very High Frequency
VLF	Very Low Frequency. Capable of use, as with the United States AABNCP, for communication with submerged submarines.
VLS	Vertical Launch System
V/STOL	Vertical/Short Take-Off and Landing

W
Warsaw Pact	Military alliance of Eastern Europe comprising seven countries which arose in response to the creation of NATO and the re-militarisation of West Germany in the 1950s.
Weapons Grade Fissile Material	Uranium or plutonium in a form capable of use in nuclear weapons.
Weapons Mix	The mix of weapons and missiles in a country's arsenal, especially when older and new weapons are in service simultaneously.
White Cloud	A US Navy radar satellite ocean-surveillance programme.
World-wide Military Command and Control System	The operational direction and support of US forces deployed throughout the World is provided through this system, which also contains the National Military Command System.

Y
Yellowcake	Uranium oxide, a bright yellow powder created following the chemical treatment of crushed rock containing uranium.
Yield	The explosive power of a nuclear weapon, expressed as an equivalent in metric tons of TNT.

Z
Zero Option	A proposal for limiting the deployment of nuclear weapons in Europe, put forward by US President Reagan.

Index

Numbers in *italics* refer to illustrations and diagrams

Unclassified current reference sources have been used for factual material throughout this book, including:

The Military Balance 1986-87 (IISS: London, 1986)
Soviet Military Power 1986-87 (US GPO, 1986-87)
Soviet Strategic Defense Programs (US GPO, 1985)